LIVING
WITH FEAR

AUGUST 2008

A POPULATION-BASED SURVEY ON ATTITUDES ABOUT PEACE, JUSTICE, AND SOCIAL RECONSTRUCTION IN EASTERN DEMOCRATIC REPUBLIC OF CONGO

PATRICK VINCK
PHUONG PHAM
SULIMAN BALDO
RACHEL SHIGEKANE

**HUMAN
RIGHTS
CENTER**
UNIVERSITY
OF
CALIFORNIA
BERKELEY

PAYSON CENTER
FOR INTERNATIONAL DEVELOPMENT

international center for
TRANSITIONAL
JUSTICE

This survey was conducted by the Berkeley-Tulane Initiative on Vulnerable Populations, a joint project of University of California, Berkeley's Human Rights Center and Tulane University's Payson Center for International Development, and the New York–based International Center for Transitional Justice.

The **BERKELEY-TULANE INITIATIVE ON VULNERABLE POPULATIONS** conducts research in countries experiencing serious violations of human rights and international humanitarian law. Using empirical research methods to give voice to survivors of mass violence, the Initiative aims to ensure that the needs of survivors are recognized and acted on by governments, UN agencies, and nongovernmental organizations. The Initiative helps improve the capacity of local organizations to collect and analyze data about vulnerable populations so that their human rights can be protected. The **HUMAN RIGHTS CENTER** investigates war crimes and serious violations of human rights and international humanitarian law. The **PAYSON CENTER** is an interdisciplinary center created to promote sustainable human development among vulnerable populations through innovative and interdisciplinary education, research, and programs.

The **INTERNATIONAL CENTER FOR TRANSITIONAL JUSTICE** is an international human rights organization that assists countries pursuing accountability for past mass atrocity or human rights abuse. The Center works in societies emerging from repressive rule or armed conflict, as well as in established democracies where historical injustices or systemic abuse remain unresolved. It operates in about 30 countries around the world, bringing to bear technical expertise and comparative experiences on transitional justice issues to partners including civil society, truth commissions or tribunals, governments, the United Nations or regional organizations, and interested individuals. ICTJ currently has offices in Bogota, Brussels, Cape Town, Geneva, Kinshasa, Monrovia, and New York, as well as presences in Beirut and Jakarta.

Research and production of *Living with Fear* were made possible by grants from the John D. and Catherine T. MacArthur Foundation, Humanity United, Swedish International Development Cooperation Agency, the European Commission, and the BBC World Service Trust.* The information provided and views expressed in this publication can in no way be taken to represent the official opinion of the funding agencies.

* The BBC World Service Trust uses media to promote development and human rights around the world. As the BBC's independent charity, it relies on the BBC's reputation, resources and expertise to implement its donor-funded projects. The Trust works in over 43 countries worldwide. As of May 31, 2008, it is working in Africa, Asia, the Middle East, former Soviet Union and Europe, using media creatively in the fields of health, livelihoods, governance, human rights and post-disaster rehabilitation.

CONTENTS

EXECUTIVE SUMMARY

Two years after the Democratic Republic of Congo (DRC) held its first elections since independence, the country is at a crossroads. Among the key challenges facing the DRC today is the question of how the country will address the massive human rights atrocities of its recent past to establish a foundation for peace and security, the rule of law, and respect for human rights to prevail in the future. The 2006 elections capped an era of international armed conflict and massive violence in the DRC that began with Laurent Desire Kabila's 1996–1997 campaign to liberate Congo from decades of repressive rule under Mobutu Sese Seko. The advent of an elected government sets the stage for state-building initiatives focusing on governance and critical long-term institutional reform in the security and justice sectors. Yet armed conflict and mass violence continue to plague eastern DRC.

This report presents the results of a population survey undertaken by the Human Rights Center (HRC) at the University of California, Berkeley, the Payson Center at Tulane University, and the International Center for Transitional Justice (ICTJ). Focusing on areas most affected by conflict in eastern DRC, surveys were conducted from September to December 2007 among a sample population of 2,620 individuals in the Ituri district in Oriental province and the provinces of North and South Kivu. The report concentrates its analysis on the survey results in eastern DRC, but comparative interviews were also conducted among a sample population of 1,133 individuals in Kinshasa and Kisangani. The survey sought to assess exposure to violence among the population; understand the priorities and needs of Congolese civilians affected by the conflicts; and capture attitudes about peace, social reconstruction, and transitional justice mechanisms.

This survey aims to give voice to the victims of the Congo conflicts and thereby urge the Congolese government and international actors engaged in DRC's post-election construction to consult the Congolese population and heed their needs and concerns in setting priorities in designing Congo's future. Acknowledging some limitations inherent in conducting a population-based survey in an environment of ongoing conflict, this survey has yielded rich results.

While the report engages in a nuanced and detailed analysis of the survey results on a wide range of topics related to population priorities, peace, security, perceptions of the origins and possible resolution of the conflict, reintegration, transitional justice mechanisms, and access to information, the survey's key **findings** are as follows:

- Human rights abuses suffered by the population of eastern DRC, including sexual violence, and fear of government soldiers and militias alike are widespread. Many respondents were interrogated or persecuted by armed groups (55%), forced to work or enslaved (53%), beaten by armed groups (46%), threatened with death (46%), or had been abducted for at least a week (34%). In eastern DRC, 23 percent witnessed an act of sexual violence, and 16 percent reported having experienced sexual violence. One-third of the respondents said they would not accept victims of sexual violence back in their community.

- The population of eastern DRC views peace (51% of respondents) and security (34%) as not only their two priorities, but also the two priorities that the Congolese government should pursue. Concerns about peace and security are followed by various social security concerns such as money (27%), education (26%), food/water (26%), and health (23%). By contrast, the populations of Kinshasa and Kisangani prioritize concerns about the economy and employment (57% and 46% in the two respective cities). Security also ranks higher as a priority in the East (34%) compared to Kisangani (22%) and Kinshasa (5%), but peace is shared as a high priority in Kisangani (56%) and the East (51%) as compared to Kinshasa (5%).

- The majority of the population of eastern DRC believes peace can be achieved in Congo (90% of respondents), defining peace primarily as national unity and togetherness (49%), the end of fear (47%), and the absence of violence (41%). The population endorses a multifaceted approach to attaining peace, including arresting those responsible for crimes (28%), through dialogue between ethnic groups (22%), dialogue with militias (22%), establishing the truth (20%), and military victory over armed groups (17%).

- The majority of the population of eastern DRC believes that justice can be achieved (80% of respondents), defining justice as establishing the truth (51%), applying the law (49%), and "being just/fair" (48%). Among the means to achieve justice, the eastern Congolese population endorses the national court system (51%), followed by the International Criminal Court (ICC) (26%), military courts (15%), and traditional/customary justice mechanisms (15%). Furthermore, there is strong desire for the international community to assist national prosecutions (82%).

- The majority of the population of eastern DRC (85% of respondents) believes it is important to hold those who committed war crimes accountable and that accountability is necessary to secure peace (82%). Among war crimes, it believes it is most important to seek accountability for those responsible for murders/killings (92%) and rape/sexual violence (70%). Among the various trial options to hold war criminals accountable, there is a clear preference for national trials (45%), followed by internationalized trials in the DRC (40%). There is little support for no trials (8%) and international trials abroad (7%). In other words, 85 percent prefers that trials be held in the DRC, whether national or internationalized trials.

- The population of eastern DRC holds a nuanced view that peace and accountability must simultaneously be pursued. Few respondents identified providing justice (2%) or arresting those responsible for violence (2%), punishing those responsible (1%) or encouraging reconciliation (1%) among their immediate priorities. However, they indicated more frequently that promoting justice should be a priority of the government, citing justice (10%) and arresting (6%) or punishing (5%) those responsible. Eighty-two percent of the same population believes that accountability is necessary to achieve peace. Furthermore, whereas 68 percent of the population would forgive war criminals if it is the only way to have peace, 62 percent of the population prefers peace with trials to hold war criminals accountable, as opposed to 38 percent of the population that prefers to endorse peace with forgiveness only.

- While there is support for the ICC as a means of achieving justice in the DRC (26% of respondents), there is low awareness among the population of eastern Congo (27%) and in Kinshasa (28%) of the ICC or of the first scheduled trial against Thomas Lubanga in eastern DRC (28%) and Kinshasa (29%). Nevertheless a majority of those in eastern DRC who had heard about the ICC would like to participate in ICC activities (67%), but only 12 percent know how to access it.

- Radio serves as the primary means of accessing information, as 54 percent of the population of eastern DRC listens to the radio on a daily basis.

These key survey results and others explored in this report should inform the Congolese government and other actors, both national and international, engaged in DRC in designing long-term programming and should inspire future efforts to consult the Congolese population in deepening an understanding of the Congolese population's concerns.

Key recommendations that emerge from the survey results include the following actions:

TO THE CONGOLESE GOVERNMENT

- Implement the recent peace negotiations addressing security concerns with belligerents in the East. In light of the destabilizing potential of ongoing conflict in eastern DRC, peace and security remain prerequisites for future economic development for the DRC.

- Undertake effective reform of the security sector, not only to ensure that past human rights violators are removed from the ranks, but also to train the national police and army to be human rights protectors rather than violators whom civilians fear, as is the current perception of the population as revealed by the survey.

- Open an inter-community dialogue to address social antagonisms, resolve underlying causes of the conflicts including access to land and exploitation of natural resources, facilitate the demobilization and reintegration of former combatants, and permit the return of internally displaced and refugees.

- Develop a broad-based reconstruction plan that engages the population and reflects the priorities expressed by the respondents.

- Commit to national dialogue with the population to assess various transitional justice mechanisms, including prosecutions and other reconciliation mechanisms, such as inter-ethnic dialogue to address root causes of the conflict.

- Engage in effective national judicial sector reform including
    - Reform of military and civilian court systems to guarantee independence, transparency, and due process to build trust in judicial system.
    - Prioritize the prosecution of war crimes and ensure national complementarity with the ICC by adopting an effective legislative framework for national prosecutions of war crimes.
    - End impunity for crimes of rape and sexual violence.

TO THE INFORMAL AND FORMAL BELLIGERENTS ACTIVE IN EASTERN DRC

- Respect the ceasefire terms of recent peace agreements and engage in an effective process of demobilization, disarmament, and reintegration. The government of Rwanda should engage in meaningful collaboration for the disarmament, demobilization, and repatriation of Rwandan Hutu combatants of the Democratic Forces for the Liberation of Rwanda (FDLR) on DRC soil.

TO BILATERAL AND MULTILATERAL INTERNATIONAL DONORS

- Maintain pressure on the DRC government and belligerents to respect the peace process; monitor and ensure respect for the ceasefire.

- Ensure that the DRC government and belligerents pursue peace and justice simultaneously by including commitments that guarantee accountability and the pursuit of a multifaceted approach to transitional justice mechanisms in ongoing peace processes.

- Focus on international engagement with national judicial sector reform to promote accountability for human rights violations and the rule of law. Transitional justice concerns should be integrated into judicial reform plans.

- Oversee government security sector reform to guarantee transitional justice concerns are met, including vetting and effective disciplinary system for ongoing human rights violations committed by army and police.

- Engage in a long-term development strategy to promote good governance of Congolese state institutions.

TO THE UN MISSION IN THE DRC (MONUC) AND UNITED NATIONS ENTITIES

- The United Nations Security Council must renew the mandate of MONUC to continue to engage in monitoring peace in eastern DRC.

- MONUC should ensure that it implements its mandate to protect civilians.

- The Office of the High Commissioner for Human Rights (OHCHR) should effectively complete its mandate to conduct a six-month mapping exercise of human rights violations and should engage in broad-based consultations of the Congolese population to seek additional information regarding the population's needs and preferences for pursuing various transitional justice mechanisms.

TO THE INTERNATIONAL CRIMINAL COURT

- Improve its information campaign and outreach for trials that will be conducted, taking advantage of radio as a means of disseminating information.

- Review the possibility of holding its trials *in situ*.

- Continue and broaden the investigation and prosecution of suspected war criminals.

INTRODUCTION

Continuous armed conflict and economic and political instability in the Democratic Republic of the Congo (DRC) pose serious challenges to achieving social reconstruction, justice, and peace. Decades of repressive autocratic rule under Mobutu Sese Seko came to an end through the violent campaign of Laurent Desire Kabila in 1997. But Kabila's new reign quickly erupted into war and de facto division of the country into rebel-controlled, foreign-occupied territories. While open armed conflict officially came to an end with the signing of a peace agreement in 2002, violence continued unabated in numerous local conflicts in the East. The wars in eastern Congo have been described as the deadliest since World War II. The International Rescue Committee and the Burnet Institute estimated that 5.4 million "excess deaths" occurred in Congo between August 1998 and April 2007.[1] Today, two years after the first democratic elections were held in the DRC since independence, local violence continues to simmer, and even flare, in the East. All sides to the conflict have committed flagrant violations of international humanitarian law, including targeting civilians for murder, rape and other forms of sexual violence; forced displacement; recruiting child soldiers; abducting civilians; looting; and damaging property. A state of near impunity exists for perpetrators with only a handful being prosecuted by the International Criminal Court (ICC) or national Congolese civil or military courts.

Despite this environment of impunity, Congo has made modest efforts to support the quest for justice. Former belligerents expressed support for justice and reconciliation and called for an end to impunity when they signed the Sun City Peace Agreement in 2002. Congo is credited with lodging the ratification that marked the entry into force of the Rome Statute establishing the ICC.[2] It made one of the first state referrals to the ICC to investigate war crimes and crimes against humanity known to

---

1. International Rescue Committee and Burnet Institute, "Mortality in the Democratic Republic of Congo: An Ongoing Crisis" (2007). However, such estimates should be interpreted with caution because they rely on assumptions about total population size and the baseline mortality level against which "excess mortality" is measured.
2. DRC signed the Rome Statute of the International Criminal Court (ICC) on 8 September 2000 and ratified it on 11 April 2002. See http://www.icc-cpi.int/asp/statesparties/country&id=5.html (accessed on 9 June 2008).

have occurred during the war and became the first investigation opened by the ICC's office of the prosecutor.[3] Since then, three Iturian warlords have been surrendered to the ICC. The ICC has also unsealed an arrest warrant for charges of crimes against humanity and war crimes in the Central African Republic against the Congolese Jean-Pierre Bemba, a Senator, former Vice President and leading opposition figure who lost the run-off in the 2006 presidential elections to Joseph Kabila.[4] The arrest warrant for Bemba was quickly executed by the Belgian authorities in May 2008. The Congolese government has also called on the United Nations (UN) to set up an ad-hoc international tribunal to rule on crimes committed before 2002.[5]

The Congolese government and other institutions, however, lack the political will, capacity, and/ or necessary resources to rebuild the nation and address both the national and local root causes of the complex conflicts in the DRC. Among the institutions specifically mandated to address past atrocities and injustices, the Truth and Reconciliation Commission that operated during the transition period leading to the 2006 elections and a National Observatory of Human Rights have been criticized as being neither credible nor effective. These institutions were established by ruling elites without consulting the victims of abuses and were dominated by former belligerents, who have insured that no credible investigations of past violations would occur. Lastly, by framing the conflict regionally with a focus on Rwanda, international peace builders failed to address other local causes of violence, such as conflict over land, exploitation of natural resources, or social antagonisms.[6]

As a result, the parties to the 2002–2007 transition and the current elected Congolese government have brought little significant change to the daily abuses to which Congolese civilians remain victim. While the conflict has been largely confined to eastern DRC over the last few years, in North Kivu in particular, the situation remains volatile and a factor of national and regional destabilization. Recent violence and subsequent negotiations, however, have spurred new hopes for a lasting peace in Congo.

3. "Prosecutor receives referral of the situation in the Democratic Republic of Congo," The Hague: ICC press release, 19 April 2004; "The Office of the Prosecutor of the International Criminal Court opens its first investigation," The Hague: ICC press release, 23 June 2004.
4. "ICC Arrest Jean-Pierre Bemba – massive sexual crimes in Central African Republic will not go unpunished," The Hague: ICC press release, 24 May 2008.
5. The ICC can only investigate crimes committed on or after it came into being, on 1 July 2002.
6. Autesserre S., "Local Violence, National Peace? Postwar 'Settlement' in the Eastern D.R. Congo (2003–2006)," African Studies Review 49/3 (2006): 1–29.

Against this backdrop of fitful transitional steps in the DRC, the Human Rights Center (HRC) at the University of California, Berkeley, the Payson Center at Tulane University, and the International Center for Transitional Justice (ICTJ), conducted a survey to document the experiences, views, and attitudes of those most affected by the conflict in the DRC.[7] In contrast to other war-affected areas in Africa, such as northern Uganda, little research exists in the case of eastern DRC. Yet the views of victims are essential to policymakers in the fields of peace negotiation, post-conflict reconstruction, and transitional justice.

The objectives of the survey were to:

1. Assess the overall exposure to violence among the population in eastern Congo as a result of war and violations of human rights and international humanitarian law since 1993.

2. Understand the priorities and needs of civilians affected by the conflict.

3. Capture attitudes about peace and social reconstruction, including resettlement, protection, unity, and the reintegration of former combatants.

4. Document attitudes and opinions about transitional justice mechanisms.

5. Elucidate views on the relationship between peace, justice, and social reconstruction.

The geographic focus of this survey captured attitudes in the three regions of eastern DRC most directly affected by war, namely the Ituri district of Oriental province and the provinces of North and South Kivu. In doing so, this survey gives voice to the perceptions and concerns of the Congolese population that has suffered and remains the most vulnerable to mass violence and human rights abuse as a result of the ongoing armed conflict in the region. This focus is reflected in the in-depth analysis of the survey results from the Ituri district, and North and South Kivu in this report. For the purposes of comparison, however, the survey also assessed opinions in Kinshasa and Kisangani. The Congo wars have had a substantially different impact in Kinshasa, the nation's capital and seat of national government, which is far removed from the worst fighting and human rights atrocities that occurred in the past and continue to affect eastern DRC. Kisangani has had a mixed experience, having been subjected to foreign occupation and intense fighting at the height of the Congo wars but having experienced greater peace than eastern DRC since the transition, thereby sharing some attributes as an urban setting more

7. HRC, Payson Center, and ICTJ have previously established a partnership to survey attitudes towards peace, justice, and reconciliation in neighboring Uganda, which, like the DRC, has experienced years of war and various attempts at establishing peace and justice to overcome the conflict. Like the situations in eastern DRC, northern Uganda is the site of an investigation by the ICC, which has issued an arrest warrant against Joseph Kony and other commanders who allegedly perpetrated war crimes in their service of the Lord's Resistance Army. The partnership between HRC, Payson Center, and ICTJ resulted in two reports: "Forgotten Voices: A Population-Based Survey on Attitudes about Peace and Justice in Northern Uganda" (July 2005) and "When the War Ends: A Population-Based Survey on Attitudes about Peace, Justice, and Social Reconstruction in Northern Uganda" (December 2007). Although similar in its objective, the survey in DRC was adapted to the local situation.

aligned with Kinshasa than eastern DRC. Several comparative results of the survey from Kinshasa and Kisangani are explored in this report.

Acknowledging the difficulties and inherent limitations of conducting a population-based opinion survey such as this one (see methodology section), the HRC, Payson Center, and ICTJ pursued this survey to encourage the Congolese government, formal and informal belligerents engaged in ongoing conflict, and international actors, including United Nations entities such as MONUC and OHCHR, multilateral and bilateral actors engaged in political and development assistance, to engage in further consultation and dialogue with the Congolese population to design and implement long-term initiatives to secure peace and security, transitional justice mechanisms, good governance, and the rule of law that responds to the population's needs. To that end, this report concludes with a detailed summary of the survey's key findings, as well as recommendations emerging from these results.

BACKGROUND:
THE CONGO CONFLICT

Decades of colonialism and oppressive national rule made Congo the scene of recurrent atrocities. The tumultuous years of power struggles and international interference that followed the country's independence from Belgium in 1960 paved the way, beginning in 1971, for nearly three decades of autocratic and corrupt rule under President Mobutu Sese Seko, during which the gradual decay of all state institutions left entire communities throughout the country to fend for themselves. The weakening of Mobutu's regime encouraged the emergence of a rebellion in eastern Congo in 1995. The movement was led by Laurent Kabila, a longtime leftist opponent of Mobutu and leader of the Alliance of Democratic Forces for the Liberation of Congo (AFDL). The AFDL launched an insurgency to topple the Mobutu regime in 1996, recruiting tens of thousands of child soldiers from local communities in the East. A "war of liberation" followed in 1996–97 when a regional alliance, spearheaded by Rwanda and Uganda, sent thousands of soldiers to support the AFDL. The campaign raised great hopes of change and renaissance throughout the country, and the AFDL made a triumphal entry in the Congolese capital in May 1997 as Mobutu fled the country.

The 1994 genocide in neighboring Rwanda of ethnic minority Tutsis by a Hutu-dominated regime fuelled the war of liberation. The genocide spilled over in the Congo when hundreds of thousands of predominantly Hutu refugees poured into its eastern provinces, among them genocidaires, remnants of the army and militia that perpetrated the genocide.[8] As the AFDL overran one Mobutu government stronghold after the other in late 1996, Rwandan forces accompanying the AFDL fighters pursued fleeing genocidaires across the border, killing thousands of civilians, mostly Hutu refugees and local Congolese in the cross fire.[9] Hutu extremist leaders and commanders who survived the chase later formed what would become the Democratic Forces for the Liberation of Rwanda (FDLR). While vowing to topple Rwanda's current Tutsi dominated government, the FDLR continues to pose major threats for civilian security in North Kivu.

8. Thomas Turner, *Congo Wars: Conflict, Myth, Reality* (London: Zed Books, 2007), 124.
9. For more details on this, see: Human Rights Watch, "Democratic Republic of the Congo, What Kabila Is Hiding: Civilian Killings and Impunity in Congo," 9/5(A) (October 1997), available at http://www.hrw.org/reports97/congo/.

Once in power, President Laurent Kabila attempted to curb the influence of his Rwandan and Ugandan allies. In response, Rwanda threw its support to the rebel Congolese Rally for Democracy (RCD)[10] from eastern Congo which was fighting to topple Kabila's government. This ignited the 1998–2002 "war of occupation," dubbed by the international media as "Africa's first World War" due to the involvement of several African countries, including Zimbabwe, Angola, and Namibia, which supported Kabila, while Rwanda and Uganda aided rebel groups seeking to topple him.

A stalemate during the conflict led to the division of the country into four administrative zones with each dependent on foreign backers for survival. The mainstream Rwandan-backed RCD-Goma controlled the two Kivus and parts of Katanga, Maniema, and Eastern Kasai provinces. The breakaway, Ugandan-backed RCD-Kisangani controlled parts of North Kivu and Oriental provinces, including the Ituri district. The competing Movement for the Liberation of Congo (MLC), also a Ugandan proxy, was the dominant force in Equateur province. The Congolese government managed to hold on to the western half of the country with the support of Angolan, Namibian, and Zimbabwean troops. The RCD factions merely fronted for an outright military occupation of the eastern half of the country by Rwandan and Ugandan troops[11] as a 2005 ruling by the International Court of Justice would determine in the case of Uganda.[12] These regional powers were as keen on politically controlling their local Congolese proxies as plundering the country's rich natural resources. Their fierce competition for stakes in Congo's political and economic future at times led to direct military confrontations between the Rwandan and Ugandan armies, as happened four times in Kisangani between 1999 and 2002, with hundreds of Congolese killed in the cross fire.[13]

All belligerents during the 1998–2002 war, including the national and foreign armies, used ethnic "Mai Mai" and self-defense militias as surrogates, exacerbating local disputes in rebel-held areas over land tenure and the control of local resources. In Ituri, the new war deepened a long-standing conflict between Lendu and Hema, and more generally, the conflict increasingly evolved along ethnic lines.[14] Rwandan and Ugandan insurgents groups based in eastern Congo, chief among them the FDLR and the Ugandan Allied Democratic Forces (ADF) repeatedly clashed with their respective national armies on Congolese soil during the 1998–2002 war.[15]

10. Known as a political-military party identified with Congolese Tutsi, as is its splinter group RCD-Goma.

11. Reyntjens F., "Briefing: the second Congo War: more than a remake," *African Affairs* 98 (1999).

12. International Court of Justice, Year 2005, 19 December 2005, Case Concerning Armed Activities on the Territory of the Congo (Democratic Republic of Congo v. Uganda), available at http://www.icj-cij.org/docket/files/116/10455.pdf.

13. Human Rights Watch, "Congo: Kisangani Residents Again Under Fire, Rwanda's Congolese Proxy Force Killing Civilians, Closing Civil Society Groups," 24 May 2002, available at http://hrw.org/english/docs/2002/05/24/congo4000.htm.

14. Reyntjens F., "Briefing: The Democratic Republic of Congo, from Kabila to Kabila," *African Affairs* 100 (2001): 311–17.

15. As the multilayered conflict raged, critics pointed out that Rwanda and Uganda continued to be among the leading recipients of international bilateral and multilateral development and military assistance in Africa, despite mounting evidence of the involvement of their armies in committing massive violations of human rights and international humanitarian law in the Congo.

After the 1998–2002 war erupted, the United Nations Security Council established a peacekeeping force, the UN Mission in the Democratic Republic of Congo (MONUC),[16] to assist in implementing the Lusaka Peace Accord signed in 1999. The Mission's mandate includes enforcing the ceasefire agreements, monitoring and reporting on the belligerents' disengagement from frontlines, assisting with the process of DDRRR (disarmament, demobilization, repatriation, resettlement, and reintegration), and facilitating the transition to democratic governance.

The prospect for peace improved following the assassination of Laurent Kabila in January 2001 and the ascendance of his son Joseph Kabila to the presidency. The subsequent Sun City peace agreement (2003) established a transitional government, under international supervision in the form of the International Committee in Support of the Transition (CIAT), that guaranteed former belligerents full control of the state and its resources while leaving representatives of civil society and other constituencies with little influence. The skewed power-sharing arrangement meant that the transitional partners had little incentive to begin the difficult tasks of resolving the root causes of Congo's recurrent conflicts, ending impunity, and instituting the rule of law and the enforcement of basic human rights.

Despite the signing of the Sun City agreement, armed conflict continued in eastern DRC, notably in the Ituri district of Oriental province and North and South Kivu. Violence erupted in Ituri during the First Congo War in 1999 between the rival Hema and Lendu ethnic groups. These two groups experienced a history of tensions over land use in Ituri, but the outbreak of conflict between these groups was fueled by proxy support from Uganda to both rival Hema and Lendu rebel leadership. As violence continued after the signing of the Sun City Agreement, first a European Union peacekeeping force led by the French intervened to halt the fighting in Ituri in June 2003, and then MONUC troops deployed and assumed peacekeeping responsibilities in Ituri in September 2003. MONUC forces have maintained a significant peacekeeping presence in Ituri ever since.

Violence also continued in North and South Kivu during the transition. The Sun City peace agreement called for the integration of the national army, a process known as "brassage," requiring soldiers from all regions to report to a central training location from where they would be deployed to regions other than those in which they had previously fought. This meant that in eastern Congo, RCD-affiliated soldiers could be placed under the command of an officer loyal to Kabila. Many RCD soldiers resisted the "brassage" program and their deployment away from their home regions. A key contributing factor in this resistance was the government's failure to investigate the killings of hundreds of soldiers from eastern Congo, many of them Congolese of Rwandan heritage, that occurred in its garrisons at the beginning of the war. General Laurent Nkunda, a notorious Rwandan-trained, Congolese Tutsi whose involvement in committing widespread rights violations and war crimes during the 1998–2002 war was well documented by Human Rights Watch and other independent rights groups, refused to deploy to Kinshasa after the war and instead commanded two RCD brigades in North Kivu.[17] He would later

16. MONUC has a Chapter VII mandate from the United Nations Security Council, authorizing it to use all necessary means within its capacities in the areas of its deployment to protect civilians from threat of violence.
17. Rwanda is known to have provided, at minimum, rhetorical support for Nkunda. Some suspect the Rwandan government provided Nkunda with arms, and others have documented occasions when Rwanda allowed Nkunda to recruit sol-

rebel and lead his soldiers in attacking government forces in the town of Bukavu, South Kivu in 2004. His rebellion continues.[18]

The transition period ended with the 2006 legislative and presidential elections and the subsequent establishment of provincial and national parliaments and the swearing-in of President Joseph Kabila in December 2006. The massive and predominately nonviolent participation of the Congolese in the electoral process sent a clear message to the political elites that the population was keen on democratic transformation and the realization of genuine reforms. However, these reforms have yet to materialize and fighting continues to rage in eastern Congo, particularly in the provinces of North and South Kivu.

The 2006 elections also brought about the demise of RCD-Goma, the main political vehicle for Congolese Tutsi and Rwandan influence. Triggered by this loss of political influence and increased anti-Tutsi rhetoric during and after the elections, Nkunda stepped up his attacks against the government, claiming he was acting to "protect" Congolese Tutsi from the FDLR and others. Nkunda consolidated his armed forces to create his own movement, the National Congress for the Defense of the People (CNDP). His forces have engaged in waves of armed assaults and clashes with the Congolese national army (FARDC) and even MONUC troops from 2004 to the present.

Seeking a way to end the conflict with Nkunda, in late 2006 the government entered into a compromise, brokered by Rwanda, that called for a limited form of military integration called "mixage," which allowed Nkunda's troops to be integrated with government forces in North Kivu. Unlike "brassage," these mixed forces were deployed locally in eastern Congo to conduct military operations against the FDLR. However, mixage failed to accomplish its goal of bringing Nkunda under the control of the government and was ended in August 2007.

Both Congolese troops and those loyal to Nkunda have committed grave violations of international humanitarian law including forced displacement and killing of civilians, abductions, recruitment of child soldiers, rape and other forms of sexual violence, and looting and destruction of property. Between 2003 and 2006, Congolese and international workers identified and removed approximately 30,000 children from the ranks of both the regular military and other armed groups and returned them to civilian life.[19] And according to the UN, in 2006, 27,000 sexual assaults were reported in South Kivu alone. In one town surveyed, 70 percent of the women reported being sexually brutalized.[20]

Other recent initiatives seeking to quell Nkunda's violent campaign include the Nairobi Communiqué, signed by the Rwandan and Congolese governments in November 2007 to disarm the FDLR, and the Goma Conference on Peace, Security, and Development in North and South Kivu in January 2008, which has resulted in a ceasefire agreement to end the military standoff in North Kivu and addresses other pressing local security issues and ethnic tensions. While local initiatives played a leading role in

diers, sometimes children, within its borders. Human Rights Watch, "Renewed Crisis in North Kivu" (October 2007), 49.

18. For more on Nkunda's role during the war, see: Human Rights Watch, "Democratic Republic of Congo, War Crimes in Kisangani: The Response of Rwandan-backed Rebels to the May 2002 Mutiny," 14:6(A) (August 2002).

19. Human Rights Watch, "Renewed Crisis in North Kivu" (October 2007), 48.

20. Jeffery Gettleman, "Rape Epidemic Raises Trauma of Congo Wars," *New York Times*, 7 October 2007.

the Goma process, the establishment of follow-up institutions, enforcement of agreements reached at the national level, implementation of much needed reforms, and FDLR demobilization still depend on decisive action by the central government. The Goma ceasefire remains fragile as a result.

In the neighboring district of Ituri, the deployment of UN peacekeepers and the disarmament of the main militias have brought about relative stability.[21] However, the failure to address impunity for the massive violations that took place during the conflict; the social, structural, and distributional injustices; the absence of state institutions; and the continued plundering of the region's rich natural resources for the benefit of a few pose serious threats of a relapse into deadly violence.

During the transition and to this day, little has been done to address impunity within the security forces and armed groups or to reform the justice sector. Despite considerable support for training and rehabilitation of the judicial infrastructure, corruption continues to be endemic, including, most insidiously, the protection of higher political interests. Furthermore, all-encompassing military jurisdiction over human rights violations has yet to be reformed.

Although the DRC is a signatory to the Rome Statute, the Statute has not yet been incorporated into domestic law. Some military tribunals, which have jurisdiction over international crimes, have brought a few cases to trial, but so far only low-ranking soldiers have been found guilty. Even when prison sentences have been handed down, the state of the penitentiary system is such that most of those convicted escape almost immediately. The referral of the situation in eastern Congo and subsequent transfer of three warlords to the International Criminal Court are welcome developments. However, to date, the cases remain limited to Ituri and the ICC jurisdiction is limited to crimes committed after 2002. At the same time, the Truth and Reconciliation Commission established by the 2002 Sun City agreement failed to achieve any of its objectives.

In short, peace, social reconstruction, justice, and reconciliation remain distant dreams in Congo. The military and other government security forces continue to be among the worst perpetrators of daily human rights violations against the population and the source of instability. Civilians remain targets of the indiscriminate violence, including killing, torture, displacement, abduction, and epidemic levels of rape and other forms of sexual violence. A state of fear prevails to this day in large swaths of the DRC.

21. International Crisis Group, "Congo: Four Priorities for Sustainable Peace in Ituri," *Africa Report* 140 (2008).

SURVEY METHODOLOGY

RESEARCH DESIGN

Researchers for this study consulted with representatives of the Congolese government, leaders of civil society, and representatives of local and international nongovernmental organizations. A discussion guideline was developed to provide context and inform the development of a population-based survey. This qualitative assessment was followed from September to December 2007 by a quantitative, cross-sectional survey of 2,620 individuals in eastern DRC and 1,133 individuals in Kinshasa and Kisangani combined.

The discussion of the survey focuses on the area most affected by conflict in the DRC: the eastern provinces of North and South Kivu and the Ituri district in the Oriental Province (North Kivu: n= 1,081, South Kivu: n=815, Ituri District: n=724). In this report, the terms "eastern Congo," "eastern DRC," or "East" refer to these three locations. The provinces of North and South Kivu, bordering Uganda, Rwanda, and Burundi, have experienced massive displacement and fierce fighting throughout the years of conflict until today. The Ituri district remains volatile and was the site of intense battles between proxy forces of the local Hema and Lendu ethnicities. For comparison, the survey also interviewed 1,133 individuals in the capital Kinshasa (n=592) and in Kisangani (n=541). Kisangani experienced intense fighting between Ugandan- and Rwandan-backed rebel groups between 1999 and 2002, but fighting subsided for the most part after the signing of the Sun City agreement in 2002. Kinshasa, on the western edge of the country, is geographically removed from the situation in eastern Congo, and residents thus hold different perspectives on the various conflicts. The survey included Kinshasa to examine differences in attitudes toward justice, peace, security, and accountability between the political center and the eastern regions.

In eastern Congo, three teams of eight to 16 local men and women, 18 years and older, each representing the ethnic group in the area under study and fluent in the local language (i.e., Swahili and Lingala), collected data using a standardized questionnaire. The interviewers participated in a four-day training session with mock interviews and piloted the survey to familiarize themselves with the questionnaire, interview techniques, and selection of respondents.

The sampling universe included all adults (18 years of age or older) living in the selected area. Respondents were selected using a multi-stage sampling strategy. In eastern Congo the levels of political divisions are "provinces," "districts," "territories," "collectivities," "groupements" (*chefferie, secteur,* urban centers), and villages. Researchers first obtained a list of all collectivities and population estimates within the provinces of North Kivu, South Kivu, and Ituri District and then used systematic random sample technique proportionate to sample size to select 30 collectivities. Within each collectivity, 25 percent of the *groupements* from a list of all *groupements* were selected. Villages were randomly selected from a list of villages established for each selected *groupements.* Population-size estimates were not available at the *groupement* and village levels. In the villages, interviewers were assigned to zones where they selected every other household in a randomly chosen direction. A household was defined as a group of people normally sleeping under the same roof and eating together. In each household, interviewers randomly selected one adult to be interviewed from a list of all eligible adults. Three attempts were made to contact a household or individual. The minimum sample size for each of the 30 collectivities selected in eastern Congo was 80. Some of the selected collectivities hosted internally displaced people at the time of the survey. The sampling procedure was similar in the urban settings (e.g., Kinshasa and Kisangani), with "quartier" being used as the primary sampling unit.

One-on-one interviews were conducted anonymously in a confidential setting. Due to the sensitivity of some of the questions, the interviewers were assigned to same-sex respondents. Oral rather than written consent was obtained due to the low education levels and high rate of illiteracy among the populations sampled. The interviewers sought oral consent by guaranteeing the respondents confidentiality and ensuring them that their names were never recorded. Respondents did not receive compensation for participating in this study. The study protocol was reviewed and approved by the Human Subject Committees of the University of California, Berkeley, Tulane University, and the University of Kinshasa, DRC.

RESEARCH INSTRUMENTS

The survey instrument covered 13 topics including (1) demographics, (2) place of living/displacement, (3) priorities and access to services, (4) sense of security, (5) sense of community, group dynamic, and reintegration, (6) understanding of peace and justice, (7) peace and mechanisms for peace, (8) accountability and mechanisms for justice, (9) the ICC, (10) truth, (11) victims and reparation, (12) psychological impact, and (13) the role of the media. (The presentation of the results does not follow this order.) The instrument was developed by a team with expertise in human rights, law, transitional justice, epidemiology, psychiatry, anthropology, surveying, and the conflict in eastern Congo, in consultation with local actors. The instrument was first developed in French and then translated into the local languages and tested. Back-translation and consultation with local experts ensured the quality of the translation. In addition to the qualitative survey, some in-depth interviews and key-informant interviews were conducted in selected sampled sites to gain an understanding of the concepts and judicial mechanisms under study.

STATISTICAL ANALYSIS

Data were entered into Microsoft Access database. They were subsequently imported and analyzed using Statistical Package for Social Science (SPSS) version 16.0. No weighting factors were used during the analysis because selection of the primary sampling unit was done proportionately to the population size

LIMITATIONS

All possible steps were taken to ensure the reliability and accuracy of the data collected. Nevertheless, some limitations to the study must be acknowledged in light of the inherent challenges of doing population-based field research in conflict and post-conflict settings.

First, recall error and the sensitivity of some questions may have affected the accuracy of respondents' answers. Although no names were recorded and confidentiality of the responses was guaranteed prior to the interviews, fear of reprisals might have influenced how candid the respondents were in providing their answers to the survey questions.

Second, respondents' perceptions and answers were subject to influence by local events that occurred contemporaneous to the survey. The survey took place at a time of renewed fighting between government forces and the troops of Laurent Nkunda in North Kivu. The data, therefore, likely reflects the local population's strong reactions to the escalation of violence and displacement. Due to security concerns, two *groupements* in the territories of Masisi and Rutshuru (where most of the violence took place) were replaced with other *groupements* randomly selected within the same respective territories. In Ituri, the survey took place just after the ICC announced the transfer of Germain Katanga to The Hague. This may have affected the views on the Court.

Third, while the survey questions were finalized after consultations with key stakeholders, respondents were free to interpret the questions according to their own perceptions of the terms used. As such, where the survey gauges attitudes towards "peace" and "security," "justice" and "accountability," "war crimes" and "truth-seeking mechanisms" for example, the respondents reacted to these questions according to their individual understanding of those terms. Such concepts were not explained to the respondents to avoid leading their answers.

Fourth, although three attempts were made to contact selected respondents, not all sampled individuals could be interviewed. A total of 649 households, or 15 percent of all the sampled households, were replaced, most frequently because no one was home (half of the cases) or because they refused (46%) and no one else could be selected. Within selected households, 412 individuals, or 10 percent of all selected individuals were replaced by another randomly selected adult of the same gender within the same household: 54 percent refused, 38 percent were not home, and 8 percent were replaced for other reasons. It is unknown whether the opinions of replaced individuals differed significantly from those of the selected respondents.

Fifth, the study was designed to provide results representative of eastern DRC, including the provinces of North Kivu and South Kivu and the Ituri district, and Kinshasa and Kisangani. The results do not therefore represent the opinion of all Congolese, although they are representative of the populations in the selected areas. Furthermore, census data available to the researchers regarding the populations under study in this survey are of limited reliability. The last census in DRC was conducted in 1984 and since then only projected population estimates are available. Probability sampling based on those population estimates was used to select respondents. This in turn may have affected the results. Nevertheless, because population estimates are relatively accurate, the results are deemed representative of the areas under study.

FINDINGS IN EASTERN DRC AND DISCUSSION

INTRODUCTION

This survey focused on capturing attitudes of the populations that have suffered the most from ongoing conflict in eastern DRC, including the Ituri district of Oriental province and the provinces of North and South Kivu. This section discusses the results of the survey in these three areas of eastern DRC. As some variance in attitudes among the residents of Ituri and North and South Kivu emerged from the survey, defining characteristics of the nature of the conflicts and recent initiatives to address local concerns in these areas are first introduced.

The Ituri district of Oriental province has been the site of historical tensions, primarily over land use, between the pastoralist Hema and agriculturalist Lendu ethnic groups. Ituri experienced intense fighting during the Second Congo War, beginning in 1999. The district was occupied by the Ugandan People's Defense Force (UPDF) but Uganda backed competing local factions resulting in repeated clashes between Hema and Lendu armed groups over the years. The Ituri district experienced an influx of small arms and the illegal exploitation of resources such as gold and timber. Despite the signing of the Sun City peace agreement in 2002 and the retreat of the UPDF, Uganda continued to back the rival warring factions and violence continued in 2003 and beyond. As massive violations of humanitarian law continued to occur in Ituri after the entry into force of the Rome Statute of the ICC on 1 July 2002 and given the Congolese government's referral of the DRC to the ICC, war crimes committed in Ituri have been the focus of the ICC's investigations, which have resulted in the issuance of four arrest warrants for Iturian warlords.

The ongoing violence in Ituri led the UN Security Council to deploy a peacekeeping force in 2003, first an interim force led by France of European Union troops and then more permanent troops under the UN's peacekeeping force, MONUC. Several MONUC peacekeepers were killed in Ituri in 2003 and 2005. The presence of MONUC's troops in Ituri played a significant role in providing security by reducing the outbreaks of violence, which allowed for the gradual return of displaced persons prior to the 2006 elections. The stabilizing presence of MONUC peacekeepers starting in 2003 allowed for international actors and the transitional Congolese government to launch various development initiatives focused in Ituri beginning around 2005. Significantly, the European Commission–sponsored project for the Restoration of the Judicial System in Eastern Congo (REJUSCO) began as a pilot initiative focused in Ituri prior to the 2006 elections. The international attention given to Ituri, in terms of peacekeeping troops, judicial sector reform, and the ICC's investigations into war crimes over the years, are important factors to consider in interpreting the survey results below.

North and South Kivu share a history of intense and complex tensions over land, ethnicity, and citizenship exacerbated by competing claims from neighboring Rwanda, Burundi, and Uganda that continue to fuel conflict to this day. The Kivus bore the brunt of the aftermath of the Rwandan genocide in 1994, forced to absorb a massive influx of Rwandan refugees, including former Hutu genocidaires who settled in the Kivus as they reorganized and rearmed.

Outbreaks of fighting in North and South Kivu have been continuous from the Second Congo War, through the transition until today between competing factions, including the Rwandan Hutu rebel movement (FDLR), the rebel movement of Laurent Nkunda (CNDP), government forces (FARDC), and various traditional Mai Mai militias. The DRC and Rwandan governments signed the Nairobi Communiqué in November 2007 agreeing on a process to demobilize, disarm, and return Rwandan Hutus back to Rwanda. But little progress has been made in implementing this agreement. Constant low-level fighting occurs in South Kivu and the conflict there is characterized by the widespread incidence of rape and sexual violence as a tool of conflict between the Mai Mai militias, FARDC, and Rwandan and Burundian rebel movements operating in the region. North Kivu has experienced more intense outbreaks of fighting than South Kivu since the 2006 elections, particularly instigated by General Nkunda's CNDP movement, resulting in massive displacement over the last two years. The January 2008 Goma agreement seeks to quell fighting, but the ceasefire has been ignored and continuous fighting and violations of humanitarian law have continued throughout 2008. Intense fighting occurred in North Kivu in 2007 during the time the survey was conducted.

SOCIO-DEMOGRAPHIC CHARACTERISTICS AND DISTRIBUTION OF THE RESPONDENTS

Using the methodology outlined above, a total of 2,620 interviews were conducted in eastern DRC with individuals randomly selected in the provinces of North Kivu (1,081 interviews), South Kivu (815 interviews), and the district of Ituri (724 interviews). The interviews were conducted in 200 villages and six urban areas randomly selected. The sample was designed so that results are representative for each of the areas under study: North Kivu, South Kivu, Ituri, Kinshasa, and Kisangani. Figure 1 illustrates the geographic distribution of the final sample in the eastern provinces.

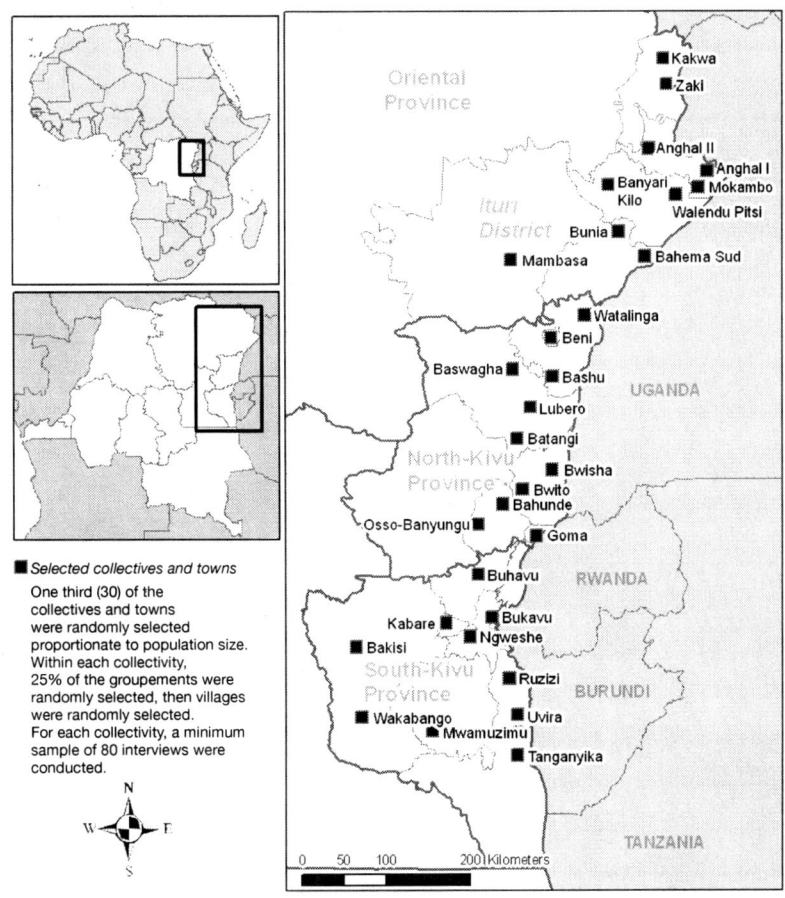

Selected collectives and towns

One third (30) of the collectives and towns were randomly selected proportionate to population size. Within each collectivity, 25% of the groupements were randomly selected, then villages were randomly selected. For each collectivity, a minimum sample of 80 interviews were conducted.

FIGURE I: GEOGRAPHIC DISTRIBUTION OF RESPONDENTS (EASTERN DRC)

The sample was selected regardless of any selection criteria with the exception that only adults aged 18 or older were to be interviewed and that same-sex interviews were to be conducted (i.e., women interviewed women and men interviewed men). As a result, the sample presents a great variety of socioeconomic characteristics and ethnicity. Overall, the sample comprises more than 80 ethnic groups, with six groups accounting for 56 percent of respondents: Nande (19%), Shi (10%), Hunde (8%), Lega (8%), Alur (7%) and Hutu (5%). Table 1 provides detail of the main ethnic groups by zone under study.

The mean age of respondents was 37 years old (median 34.0, S.D. 13.6). Most respondents described themselves as married or in a marital relationship (72%, including 9% in a polygamous relationship), and the average household size was 6.8 (median 6.0, S.D. 3.6). Most respondents lived in households that had children (90%) and 78 percent had their own children. Regarding religion, most respondents described themselves as Catholic (49%), Protestant (34%), or Muslim (5%).

	North Kivu	South Kivu	Ituri	Total
Sample size (n)	1,081	815	724	2,620
Gender (% female)	49.7	49.6	49.7	49.7
Mean Age (S.D.)	36.9 (13.3)	34.9 (12.8)	38.2 (14.7)	36.6 (13.6)
Ethnicity*				
Alur (%)	--	--	23.3	6.5
Bembe (%)	--	7.4	0.1	2.3
Fulero (%)	--	11.8	--	3.7
Hema (%)	--	--	13.4	3.7
Hunde (%)	19.1	0.1	--	7.9
Hutu (%)	12.0	0.5	--	7.9
Kakwa (%)	--	--	10.5	2.9
Lega (%)	1.3	22.9	0.1	7.7
Lendu (%)	.01	--	13.3	3.7
Lugbara (%)	--	--	11.2	3.1
Nande (%)	42.5	0.6	4.3	18.9
Shi (%)	1.4	30.3	.04	10.1
Other (%)	23.6	26.4	23.3	24.4

* Ethnic groups are provided by alphabetical order. Only groups that represented 5% or more of the respondents in any of the three regions are provided.

Respondents had generally completed little or no formal education: 22 percent had not attended any school, 19 percent had some primary education, and 14 percent completed primary education only. Over a quarter (26%) had some but incomplete secondary education. Two-thirds (66%) self-reported being able to write a simple sentence like, "it is hot today." Most respondents live by agriculture and husbandry (60%), day labor (10%), or small commercial activity (11%), and generate only meager incomes from those activities. Over 93 percent of the sampled individuals reported income below US$2/day and 85 percent had income below US$1/day; 22 percent reported no income. Most (71%) judged their income insufficient to sustain their livelihoods.

PRIORITIES AND SECURITY

Priorities

Among the survey's primary objectives was to understand respondents' priorities for moving forward toward reconstruction and development. Specifically, the survey asked respondents to evaluate their quality of life and identify, by order of importance, their top three current priorities and what they believed should be the top three priority areas of the government and the international community.

Respondents in eastern DRC generally felt their quality of life was getting worse. Only 13 percent ranked their current quality of life as good or very good, and most felt their lives currently were the same (42%) or worse (39%) compared to before the 2002 peace agreement, and the same (51%) or worse (31%) compared to before the 2006 presidential elections. This perceived deterioration indicates a generally pessimistic outlook. Nevertheless, over two-thirds of respondents believed the government was working to bring security (72%) and peace (74%) in eastern Congo. Fewer believed the government was working to improve their lives (56%) and less than half believed that the government was fighting corruption (44%) and impunity (48%).

Peace (51%) and security (34%) were the most frequently reported priorities, followed by livelihood concerns, including money (27%), education (26%), and food and water (26%). These priorities highlight the fact that security is yet to be achieved in eastern Congo and basic needs remain unsatisfied for most, against a backdrop where 93 percent of the sampled individuals reported income below US$2/day.

FIGURE 2: EASTERN DRC RESPONDENTS' TOP PRIORITIES

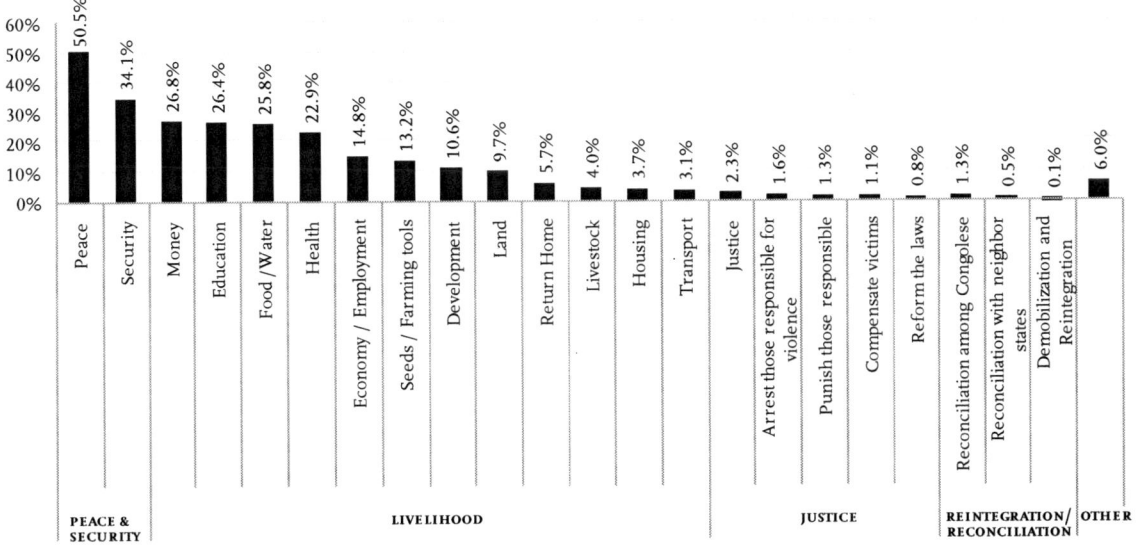

Consistent with findings from prior comparable research,[22] justice, reintegration, and reconciliation are not major priorities among respondents when peace and security are not yet met and basic needs are not satisfied. With their immediate priorities set on these goals, few respondents identified providing justice (2%) or arresting those responsible for violence (2%), punishing those responsible (1%), or encouraging reconciliation (1%) as their most pressing concerns.

In terms of what respondents thought should be the priorities of the government (the survey did not specify what level of government, whether local, provincial, or central), peace (45%) and security (42%) were once again most frequently identified. In the context of this question, only one in ten considered that promoting justice should be a priority of the government, citing justice (10%) and arresting (6%) or punishing (5%) those responsible. Among livelihood priorities, social services were most important, including education (32%), development (21%), and health (19%). Food and water, and to a lesser extent, money and the economy/employment, were mentioned as government priorities compared to respondents' own priorities.

FIGURE 3: WHAT SHOULD BE THE TOP PRIORITIES OF THE CONGOLESE GOVERNMENT?

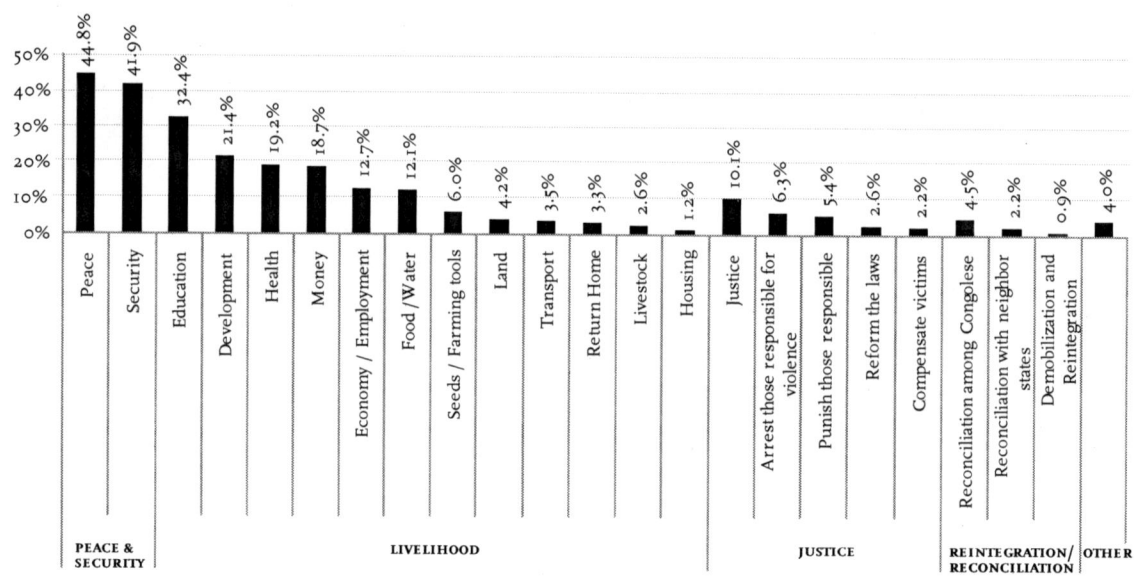

When asked what the priorities of the international community should be, respondents in eastern DRC most frequently saw it as a provider of assistance. Respondents listed most frequently that development (36%), money or income (28%), and food/water (23%) should be among the interna-

22. Pham PN, Vinck P, Stover E, Moss A, Wierda M, Bailey R, "When the War Ends. A Population-Based Survey on Attitudes about Peace, Justice, and Social Reconstruction in Northern Uganda," Human Rights Center, University of California, Berkeley; Payson Center for International Development, Tulane University; International Center for Transitional Justice, New York (December 2007).

tional community's priorities. Respondents viewed the international community's role as providing assistance rather than peace and security, which were more often cited as priorities for the Congolese government (see Figures 2 and 3), despite the mandate and presence of MONUC[23] forces in eastern DRC. This could mean that respondents either viewed MONUC forces as being ineffective at providing peace and security, held traditional views of the international community as assisting development, or that Congolese believe that it is the responsibility of the Congolese government and actors to stop fighting and provide peace and security themselves.

FIGURE 4: WHAT SHOULD BE THE TOP PRIORITIES OF THE INTERNATIONAL COMMUNITY?

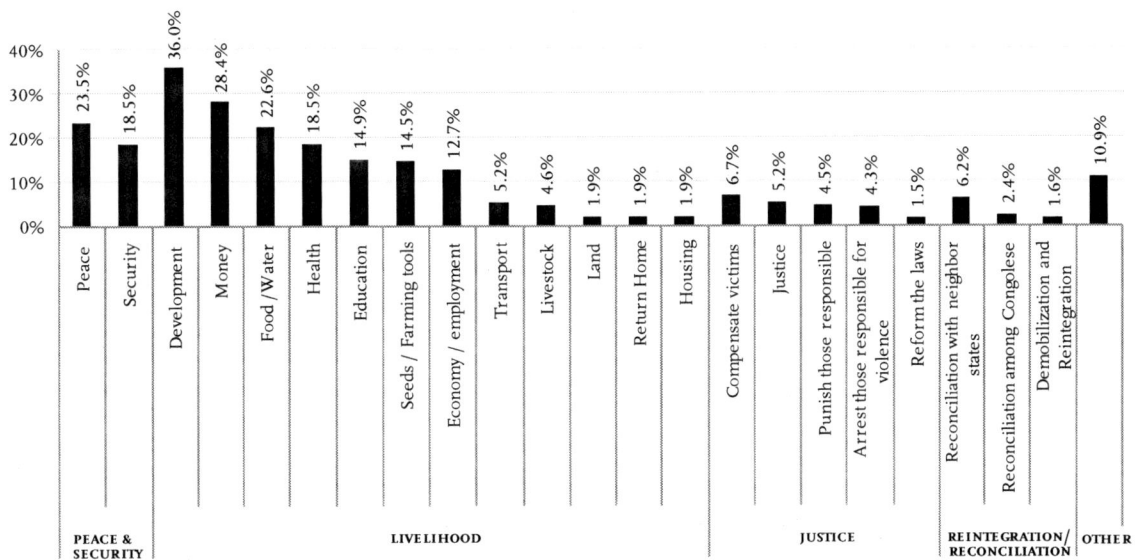

Security

In light of ongoing armed conflict, the population of eastern DRC experiences the lack of security by fearing for their individual safety and physical integrity in their daily lives. Most respondents in eastern DRC cited security, or the lack of fighting, as among their own top priorities (34%); furthermore, 42 percent of respondents in eastern DRC believed security should be a priority of the government, and 19 percent believed it should be a priority of the international community. These figures reflect both the ongoing fighting at the time of the survey and the volatility of the situation in eastern Congo. To

23. Established by the United Nations Security Council Resolution 1565 (1 October 2004) to facilitate the implementation of the Lusaka Accord signed in 1999, MONUC is authorized "to use all means deemed necessary, within the limits of its capacities and in the areas of deployment of its armed units, to protect civilians under imminent threat of physical violence; and to contribute to the improvement of the security conditions." It is one of the UN's largest peacekeeping missions.

examine the security situation further, respondents in eastern DRC were asked to rank their sense of safety in a range of situations.

Unsurprisingly, respondents in South Kivu and Ituri felt safer, on average, than those in North Kivu for all the proposed situations. This reflects the ongoing battles involving the FDLR, the troops of Laurent Nkunda, and governmental troops (FARDC) in North Kivu at the time of the survey. Generally, respondents felt least safe when meeting soldiers or armed groups (22% felt safe or very safe), reflecting the chaos and impending threat of multiple belligerent forces and the difficulties that the country is facing in reforming its security sector. Respondents also felt unsafe when meeting strangers (39%), and walking at night (38%). Thirty percent felt unsafe talking openly about their experience during the conflict, which may not only indicate a general distrust but also unresolved psychological fears. Globally, the lack of perceived safety seems to affect normal functioning of individuals and also the society as a whole.

TABLE 2: SENSE OF SAFETY

Sense of safety (% of respondents who felt safe or very safe in the following situation)	North Kivu	South Kivu	Ituri	Total
Going to nearest market (%)	38.0	73.7	73.2	58.9
Going to the field, fetch wood or water (%)	29.7	73.0	64.4	52.7
Going to nearest town / village (%)	28.7	69.1	60.8	50.1
Sleeping at night (%)	20.5	67.7	72.1	49.5
Meeting policemen (%)	27.8	54.0	62.0	45.4
Meeting people from another ethnic group (%)	27.2	55.7	60.6	45.3
Meeting strangers (%)	18.1	53.3	55.7	39.4
Walking at night in village (%)	17.4	58.0	47.8	38.4
Talking openly about your experience during the conflict (%)	14.1	44.0	39.1	30.3
Meeting soldiers / armed groups (%)	6.8	34.5	30.8	22.0

The survey further asked respondents who, in their view, protected them (see Table 3). (Respondents could provide only one response.) One-third of all respondents in eastern DRC said the national Congolese army (FARDC) protected them and about a third of respondents said "God/Jesus" (31%) or "nobody" (6%) protected them. The survey included "God/Jesus" as a choice here for several reasons. For one, the Congolese population is religious, with the majority being Catholic or Protestant. The survey results on this question may reflect the respondents' religious faith. The strong showing on this question, however, may also reflect the respondents' lack of faith or fatalism, after years of violent conflict, that the Congolese government and other belligerents are committed to protecting civilians. The lack of faith in actors' intentions to protect them when violence is widespread is illustrated by the differences between North Kivu, where open conflict raged as the survey was conducted, and Ituri, where armed conflict has been successfully contained by MONUC peacekeepers and the relatively successful deployment of government forces in the region. In North Kivu, 44 percent believed God protected them, but only 26 percent believed the national army protected them. In comparison, in Ituri 16 percent of the respondents believed God protected them and 50 percent believed the national army protected them.

Although part of MONUC's mandate is to ensure the protection of civilians, only about one in twenty respondents (4%) indicated MONUC provided them with protection. This may reflect that MONUC is either perceived as not having fulfilled its mandate of bringing security to the people, or that it is not sufficiently present in the field, especially in remote areas. This figure also correlates to the findings on priorities reflecting that only one-fifth of respondents in eastern DRC believe it should be a priority of the international community to provide security.

TABLE 3: PROTECTION

In your opinion, who protects you? (one answer)	North Kivu	South Kivu	Ituri	Total
National Congolese Army (%)	25.4	42.3	50.2	37.8
God / Jesus (%)	44.0	28.1	15.9	31.3
Police (%)	8.1	11.9	15.3	11.3
Nobody (%)	6.9	6.8	3.8	6.0
MONUC (%)	6.2	1.2	4.7	4.2
Central government, Kabila (%)	3.8	3.6	1.9	3.2
Family, friends (%)	2.1	4.8	1.4	2.7
Local government (%)	1.3	0.1	5.7	2.2
Other (%)	1.3	0.4	0.7	0.8
Militias, rebel groups (%)	0.4	0.7	0.4	0.5

PERCEPTION OF THE CONGO WARS AND EXPOSURE TO VIOLENCE

Perceptions of Origins of the Conflicts

The conflicts in eastern Congo are rooted in a variety of complex and interlinked causes. The survey asked respondents what, in their opinion, are the main origins of the conflicts. Almost one in two respondents attributed the conflicts to power/politics (47%), showing disillusionment with politics and politicians. Other frequent answers included the exploitation of natural resources (37%), land issues (35%), and ethnic divisions (29%), which are all well-known causes of the conflicts in eastern Congo. A noticeable regional difference concerns Ituri, where land disputes were seen as a cause of the conflicts by 60 percent of the respondents, while conflicts over power, politics, and natural resources were less frequently identified.

In all three regions, problems of nationality (15%) and the relationship with Rwanda (5%), including the influx of refugees after the 1994 genocide and Rwandan support for rebel groups, were also mentioned. This perception that local conflicts may be, in part, a result of spillovers from neighboring Rwanda are rooted in the history of conflict dynamics in the region. Threats to the citizenship rights of minority Congolese Tutsis during the waning years of Mobutu's regime account for their significant role in the 1996–97 AFDL rebellion, which they helped found and lead to victory under Laurent Kabila. Members of the same community dominated the main faction of the RCD rebellion during the 1998–2002 conflict, drawing massive military support and intervention from Rwanda. RCD's identification with an occupying foreign army accounts for the lack of popularity it enjoyed in eastern Congo and was a leading factor in its electoral defeat in the 2006 elections. The predominance of Tutsis in the elite units of the RCD army explains the subsequent difficulty of integrating them in Congo's new army (FARDC) because they resisted deployment away from their communities. The other pole of Rwandan-related factors concerns the destabilizing role of the FDLR as a threat to Rwanda and the Tutsi community, which General Nkunda continues to use to justify his rebellion and which Rwanda has invoked to justify its massive military support during the 1998–2002 conflict and could still invoke if appropriate circumstances arose to intervene militarily in the DRC for the third time.

TABLE 4: ORIGINS OF CONFLICTS

In your opinion, what are the origins of the conflicts in eastern Congo?	North Kivu	South Kivu	Ituri	Total
Conflicts over power (%)	48.9	50.2	39.8	46.8
Exploitation of natural resources (%)	39.0	42.2	26.7	36.6
Conflicts over land / access to land (%)	24.8	24.5	60.1	34.5
Ethnic divisions (%)	25.6	23.7	39.8	28.9
Ignorance of people (%)	13.0	12.5	11.9	12.5
Rwanda (%)	4.7	7.1	3.0	5.0
International community (%)	1.0	0.7	1.4	1.0
Problems with nationality (%)	13.5	15.6	14.6	14.5
Poverty (%)	10.7	13.1	12.2	11.9
Other (%)	7.9	8.1	6.1	7.4
Don't know (%)	2.9	3.1	1.7	2.6

Affected Populations

The human cost of the conflicts in the DRC is known to be extremely high, and goes well beyond the death of many civilians. The survey documents this, as more than four out of five respondents (81%) identified themselves as victims of the conflicts since 1993.[24] When asked to identify victims of the con-

24. The recall period of nearly 15 years (1993–2007) was used to capture the overall exposure to violence among respondents.

flicts in eastern Congo since 1993, again more than four out of five (86%) identified the population in general, using terms such as "the community," "all the people," or "everyone," showing the perceived widespread character of victimization.[25] Specific categories were particularly identified by respondents: women were perceived by almost half of the respondents as having been particularly victimized (44%). Surprisingly, in areas where the forced recruitment of children by different armed groups has reportedly been widespread (and form the basis for proceedings against Thomas Lubanga at the ICC) children were only mentioned as a victimized category by a third of respondents (33%), while elderly people were also widely perceived to have been affected (21%). By contrast, only a few respondents (2%) identified one or more specific ethnic groups as the only victims. This is surprising when correlated with the fact that 29 percent saw ethnic divisions as one of the main causes of conflicts. It indicates that, although some of the conflicts may have been caused by ethnic tensions, all groups ultimately suffered. In sum, most respondents perceived the violence as very widespread in nature and recognized the endemic use of sexual and gender-based violence and forced recruitment of children.

Displacement

Displacement is a very common feature of the conflicts in eastern Congo. The sampling included communities hosting internally displaced people, and, where appropriate, camps were included in the list of villages before random selection. About 81 percent reported they have been displaced at least once since 1993. Those most affected were in North Kivu, where one in three respondents (33%), remained displaced at the time of the survey, reflecting the ongoing fighting. Ituri was overall less affected, as displacement was least frequently reported there, still affecting three-quarters of the population.

Also, while those displaced in Ituri indicated having been displaced on average 2.5 times, those in South Kivu had been displaced 3.3 times and those in North Kivu 3.7 times. The survey confirms a pattern of multiple displacements, often to nearby areas, where the displaced are primarily hosted in the community (i.e., by friends or family members): less than half of those who were displaced at least once went to a displacement camp. This pattern made it all the more challenging to register and provide assistance to those displaced.

TABLE 5: DISPLACEMENT

	North Kivu	South Kivu	Ituri	Total
Were you ever displaced since 1993? (% yes)	81.0	85.5	75.4	80.9
How many times were you displaced? (mean)	3.7	3.3	2.5	3.3
Do you live in a camp for displaced people? (% yes)	45.6	53.3	45.4	47.9
Are you currently displaced? (% yes)	33.2	8.5	12.0	19.9

25. Respondents had the possibility to provide several answers. Percentages may not add up to 100%

Among those who were displaced at the time of the survey, the overwhelming cause of displacement for those in Ituri and North Kivu was armed conflict (90% in Ituri and 88% in North Kivu). While armed conflict was also the main cause of displacement in South Kivu (60%), one out of four respondents there cited "forced displacement" as its reason (answer options were not provided and the questions were left for the interpretation of the respondents). Respondents in Ituri identified social and/or ethnic tensions as a cause of displacement much more frequently (23%) than those in North Kivu (11%) and South Kivu (2%).

TABLE 6: CAUSES OF DISPLACEMENT

What was the reason for displacement?	North Kivu	South Kivu	Ituri	Total
Armed conflict (%)	88.2	59.7	89.5	84.0
Forced displacement (%)	16.0	27.4	15.8	17.7
Social / Ethnic Tensions (%)	10.5	1.6	22.8	10.8
Politics (%)	7.3	11.3	15.8	9.1
Natural disaster / Environmental degradation (%)	7.7	1.6	15.8	7.9
Economic reasons (%)	5.2	12.9	10.5	7.1
Problems with property (%)	5.2	3.2	7.0	5.2
Other (%)	2.4	1.6	3.5	2.5

Four of five (80%) displaced respondents stated that they would return to their villages when the security situation improved. While only few respondents in North Kivu (5%) and Ituri (2%) would never return to their place of origins, 19 percent of those in South Kivu reported that they would never return. One out of five respondents in Ituri did not know whether and when they would return.

TABLE 7: RETURN

When are you planning to return?	North Kivu	South Kivu	Ituri	Total
When there is security (%)	87.7	65.5	60.3	80.2
Never (%)	4.9	19.0	1.7	6.5
Within 1 month (%)	0.7	6.9	12.1	3.4
Within 6 months (%)	1.1	1.7	3.4	1.6
Other / Don't know (%)	5.6	6.9	22.4	8.3

Land Issues

For 35 percent of respondents, land or access to land was identified as one of the origins of the conflicts in eastern Congo. The survey asked respondents about their access to and ownership of farming land. No distinction was made between land for plant production and land for raising cattle. Two-thirds of respondents said they owned or had access to agricultural land. Among them, 24 percent faced problems regarding ownership or access, the main problems being conflict with neighbors (37%) and conflicts with an alleged owner (31%). It is interesting to note that about twice as many respondents cited conflicts with neighbors as the source of land conflict (56%) in Ituri as in North Kivu (27%). While the overall results indicate that reform of land tenure rights must be addressed, the results for Ituri support focused interventions in that district on inter-communal reconciliation and conflict resolution regarding land issues.

Most respondents who experienced problems over land tenure took action to solve the problem (70%), usually seeking support from the village authorities (39%) or customary leaders (37%).

TABLE 8: CONFLICTS OVER LAND

If experienced conflict, what type?	North Kivu	South Kivu	Ituri	Total
Conflict with neighbor (%)	26.5	35.6	56.3	36.8
Conflict with an alleged owner (%)	31.4	28.7	32.0	30.8
Land sold without permission (%)	15.7	15.8	15.5	15.7
Conflict with municipality (%)	12.4	19.8	12.6	14.4
Inaccessible due to conflict (%)	12.4	9.9	8.7	10.8
Conflict with returnees or newcomers (%)	8.6	12.9	8.7	9.8
Land illegally used by someone (%)	4.3	7.9	9.7	6.7
Conflict with other public structures (%)	7.0	5.9	5.8	6.4
Conflict with private builder (%)	9.2	4.0	3.9	6.4
Landmines (%)	4.9	1.0	3.9	3.6
Conflict with family (%)	4.3	3.0	0.0	2.8
Payment of fee (%)	5.9	0.0	0.0	2.8
Other (%)	8.1	5.0	19.4	10.3

Exposure to Violence

Respondents were asked if they experienced various exposures to trauma over the course of the conflicts in eastern Congo.[26] The majority of respondents reported having lacked basic needs such as water and food (87%), health care when needed (83%), and housing (74%).[27] They also reported the looting of cattle (76%), destruction or confiscation of their houses (66%) or land (54%), and the destruction and looting of other goods (83% and 86%, respectively).

TABLE 9: LACK OF BASIC NEEDS AND GENERAL EXPOSURE TO VIOLENCE

Have you experienced any of the following as a consequence of the conflicts in eastern Congo since 1993?	North Kivu	South Kivu	Ituri	Total
Lack water or food (%)	85.3	88.6	88.0	87.1
Lack housing (%)	74.7	79.7	67.6	74.4
Lack access to health care when sick (%)	83.2	86.1	80.2	83.3
Have your house destroyed or confiscated (%)	65.5	71.7	61.1	66.2
Have cattle, livestock stolen (%)	77.7	81.9	66.3	75.9
Have land stolen / confiscated (%)	53.2	59.6	50.3	54.4
Have other goods destroyed	84.2	87.4	76.6	83.1
Have other goods stolen	88.4	89.2	77.7	85.8

As the table below reveals, respondents in eastern DRC very frequently experienced direct exposure to violence. About half of them had been interrogated or persecuted by armed groups (55%), threatened with death (46%), or beaten by armed groups (46%). Many respondents reported having been abducted for at least a week during the course of the conflicts (34%), forced to carry loads (53%), or forced to work or enslaved (53%).[28] This very high rate could be explained by the close relationship between

26. A 15-year recall period was used to cover the period starting just before the 1994 genocide in Rwanda and subsequent arrival of Rwandan refugees.

27. According to the International Rescue Committee and the Burnet Institute's recent mortality survey from January 2006 to April 2007, only 0.4% of all deaths in DRC are directly attributed to violence. The remainder, 99.6%, are due to infectious diseases, malnutrition, and neonatal- and pregnancy-related conditions. They attributed this to disruption of health services, food insecurity, deterioration of infrastructure, and population displacement. See International Rescue Committee and Burnet Institute, "Mortality in the Democratic Republic of Congo: An Ongoing Crisis" (2007).

28. This is higher than the rate found in northern Uganda, where abduction has been associated with the forced recruitment of soldiers by the Lord's Resistance Army. See Pham PN, et al., "When the War Ends. A Population-Based Survey on Attitudes about Peace, Justice, and Social Reconstruction in Northern Uganda," Human Rights Center, University of California, Berkeley; Payson Center for International Development, Tulane University; International Center for Transitional Justice, New York (2007) and Pham PN, Vinck P, Stover E, "The Lord's Resistance Army and Forced Conscription in Northern Uganda," Human Rights Quarterly 30/2 (May 2008): 404–11.

the conflict, control over portions of the territory by armed groups, and the exploitation of the natural resources, notably mines, in such territory. Many armed groups are known to have abducted people, and forced them to work, carrying loads, so as to exploit the natural resources located in the portion of the territory they controlled. Almost half of those surveyed had family members abducted (48%) and even more had family members that went missing at some point during the conflicts (60%). The current status of family members that had gone missing was not assessed. Respondents included combatants and former combatants: about one out of eight respondents (13%) said they had fought or participated actively in combat; about half of those said they had been forced to do so (7%). On average, the level of violence appeared to be highest in South Kivu, followed by North Kivu and Ituri.

TABLE 10: PHYSICAL VIOLENCE AND FORCED CONSCRIPTION

Have you experienced any of the following as a consequence of the conflicts in eastern Congo since 1993?	North Kivu	South Kivu	Ituri	Total
Disappearance of one or more household members (%)	60.4	63.5	56.9	60.4
Being interrogated / persecuted by armed groups (%)	54.6	60.2	50.7	55.3
Being forced to work, enslaved (%)	50.8	58.1	50.3	52.9
Being forced to carry loads (%)	50.8	57.7	50.4	52.8
Have a household member abducted (%)	45.2	55.4	41.8	47.5
Being beaten by armed groups (%)	46.6	50.7	40.5	46.2
Being threatened with death (%)	43.9	51.7	42.9	46.1
Being tortured (%)	34.0	38.8	34.8	35.7
Being abducted for at least a week (%)	30.8	39.8	31.2	33.7
Being wounded because of a weapon / armed combat (%)	28.5	35.5	31.8	31.6
Being arrested, sent to jail/prison (%)	29.0	37.7	27.3	31.2
Fight, participate actively in combat (%)	9.8	18.6	10.4	12.7
Being forced to fight, participate actively in combat (%)	6.3	6.1	7.8	6.7

While this survey was not designed to provide mortality estimates, it asked respondents about deaths in their household and among family and friends. Overall, 42 percent reported the violent death of a household member, and 61 percent reported the violent death of other family members or friends.

Have you experienced any of the following as a consequence of the conflicts in eastern Congo since 1993?	North Kivu	South Kivu	Ituri	Total
Violent death of a household member (%)	36.7	45.3	44.8	41.6
Violent death of another family member or friend (%)	62.1	64.0	56.6	61.2
Death in family because of disease or malnutrition (%)	56.9	57.9	51.9	55.9

The conflicts in DRC have been accompanied by extremely high rates of rape and sexual violence.[29] Rape and sexual violence are typically underreported due to the stigma and shame involved, making it particularly difficult to assess its prevalence. The survey asked respondents several questions regarding "sexual violence," purposely leaving the term "sexual violence" undefined.[30] Nearly one out of four respondents (23%) said they had witnessed sexual violence. As many as 16 percent of respondents reported having been sexually violated, several respondents multiple times (12%). The frequency of exposure to sexual violence was similar among men and women. In-depth discussions indicated that, in addition to direct exposure to sexual violence, men who reported sexual violence may have been referring to their wives' or daughters' experience or the fact that they were forced to witness such acts.

The survey results reveal that the situation in South Kivu is even graver than in the other surveyed regions, confirming reports of the high prevalence of rape and sexual violence as a tool of conflict in South Kivu.[31] Over 20 percent of the respondents had been sexually violated (22%), often several times (18%), and over 30 percent witnessed sexual violence (30%).

Many of the victims of sexual violence are victimized twice, for they face rejection from their household or community after being victims of sexual violence. Overall, over 14 percent reported being rejected from their household or community after being victim of sexual violence (15%). Again, this was even worse in South Kivu, where over 20 percent suffered such rejection (21%)

29. Doctors Without Borders, "Democratic Republic of Congo: Rape as a Weapon in North Kivu," *MSF-USA: Field News*, 19 July 2006. According to the United Nations, 27,000 sexual assaults were reported in 2006 in South Kivu Province alone. In the town of Shabunda, Maltaiser International found that 70 percent of the women reported being sexually brutalized. See Jeffery Gettleman, "Rape Epidemic Raises Trauma of Congo War," *New York Times*, 7 October 2007.
30. Respondents' understanding may therefore vary and may or not be limited to rape.
31. "Report of the Special Rapporteur on violence against women, its causes and consequences, Yakin Ertürk: Mission to the Democratic Republic of Congo," UN Doc A/HRC/7/6/Add.4 (28 February 2007).

TABLE 12: SEXUAL VIOLENCE

Have you experienced any of the following as a consequence of the conflicts in eastern Congo since 1993?	North Kivu	South Kivu	Ituri	Total
Being witness to sexual violence (%)	21.9	30.7	17.2	23.4
Being sexually violated (%)	13.4	22.4	11.6	15.7
Being sexually violated multiple times (%)	8.5	18.4	8.7	11.6
Being rejected from your household or community after being victim of sexual violence (%)	11.7	21.2	12.3	14.8

The survey results suggest that reintegration of victims of sexual violence into their communities and families is problematic. Three out of four respondents said they would accept victims of sexual violence returning to their community or household. In other words, a quarter or more of the respondents would not accept victims of sexual violence back in their community or family. Fewer (65%) said they would accept the return of such a victim who had a child as the result of the violence.

TABLE 13: REINTEGRATION OF VICTIMS OF SEXUAL VIOLENCE

	North Kivu	South Kivu	Ituri	Total
Would you accept a victim of sexual violence back into your community? (% yes)	73.8	76.9	75.6	75.3
Would you accept a victim of sexual violence back into your household? (% yes)	72.5	76.4	75.1	74.5
Would you accept a victim of sexual violence back into your household if she had a child as the result of the violence? (% yes)	64.1	65.8	63.9	64.6

PEACE, UNITY, AND REINTEGRATION

Peace

Respondents were asked about their views on peace. A majority (90%) believed peace could be achieved. Respondents defined peace not only as the absence of violence (41%) and the end of fear (47%), but also in terms of unity, togetherness (49%) and, less frequently, socioeconomic dimensions such as achieving justice (20%) and obtaining work or money (16%), better health services (10%) or better education (8%).

TABLE 14: DEFINITION OF PEACE

In your opinion, what is peace?	North Kivu	South Kivu	Ituri	Total
Living together, united, reconciled (%)	44.4	47.3	57.4	48.9
No more fear (%)	45.8	46.6	49.3	47.0
Absence of violence (%)	46.8	39.8	32.6	40.7
Having justice (%)	23.9	19.2	15.1	20.0
Having all you need (%)	15.8	14.8	24.9	18.0
Having work, money (%)	14.9	15.5	19.3	16.3
Returning home (%)	12.9	13.2	17.7	14.3
Better health services (%)	9.7	10.0	12.0	10.4
Better education (%)	6.2	5.0	13.3	7.8
Demobilization of militias (%)	3.5	3.6	8.1	4.8
Freedom (%)	2.1	1.7	1.4	1.8
Joy, love, happiness (%)	0.9	1.0	2.6	1.4
Other (%)	10.3	9.0	4.8	8.4
Don't know (%)	0.6	0.6	0.6	0.6

When asked who, in their opinion, could bring peace to eastern Congo, 86 percent mentioned the government. The community itself was mentioned by 35 percent (the second most frequent answer) as the source responsible for bringing peace. MONUC and the international community were mentioned by 13 percent and 21 percent of respondents.

The survey then asked if respondents believed the actors they saw as responsible for bringing peace were committed to achieving it. More than half the respondents (58%) answered positively.

When asked what needed to be done to achieve peace, respondents provided a wide range of answers, such as a military victory over the armed groups (17%), arresting those responsible for crimes (28%), dialogue with the militias (22%) and ethnic groups (22%), and establishing the truth (20%).

In your opinion, who can bring durable peace in eastern Congo?	North Kivu	South Kivu	Ituri	Total
Government (%)	82.4	84.6	91.6	85.6
Community / population (%)	32.8	33.8	39.6	35.0
International community* (%)	23.6	18.8	20.6	21.3
God (%)	17.5	13.6	6.2	13.2
MONUC (%)	11.8	13.5	12.6	12.6
Rwanda (%)	6.7	7.1	4.8	6.3
Religious leaders (%)	4.8	6.1	7.8	6.1
Militia leaders (%)	6.4	3.9	5.4	5.3
Customary / Traditional leaders (%)	2.1	3.5	8.0	4.2
Uganda (%)	3.6	4.5	3.5	3.8
Representatives of ethnic groups (%)	2.5	3.9	4.9	3.6
Opposition parties (%)	2.1	2.0	4.9	2.9
Other (%)	3.5	2.9	2.8	3.1

* The answer 'international community' covers responses such as the international community, Western countries, the UN, and the like.

Unity

Living together or being united was the most frequent definition of peace among respondents (49%). Given the perceived deep divisions among the Congolese population along ethnic, political, and social identities,[32] the survey asked respondents a series of questions regarding their relations with other groups.

Three-quarters of respondents ranked as good or very good their relation with their family (74%), neighbors (77%), and community (77%). Relations with other ethnic groups were less frequently ranked as very good or good (60%), especially in North Kivu (52%).

Respondents in Ituri rated their relations with their neighbors as being very good in response to this question, but at the same time, many Ituri respondents who experienced problems over land cited serious conflicts with their neighbors as the source of conflict (see Land Issues Section, p. 31). This could indicate that Congolese individuals might be able to confine conflicts with their neighbors on certain issues, such as land, and still be able to develop communal relations with them on other fronts.

32. Hans Romkema, "Update on the DRC Transition: The Case of the Kivu Provinces," Pretoria: Institute for Security Studies (2004); S. Autesserre, "Local Violence, National Peace? Postwar 'Settlement' in the Eastern D.R. Congo (2003–2006)," *African Studies Review* 49/3 (December 2006): 1–29.

How would you rank the following (% Very good – Good)	North Kivu	South Kivu	Ituri	Total
Relations with family (%)	65.7	82.4	76.3	73.8
Relations with neighbors (%)	70.9	83.8	79.2	77.2
Relations with community (%)	71.4	82.2	79.3	77.0
Relations with other ethnic groups (%)	52.0	67.4	64.3	60.2

The survey then asked respondents to rank their level of comfort in a range of situations in the presence of members of any other ethnic group. Results varied depending on the situation, with respondents most frequently comfortable in the presence of members of any other ethnic groups in non-committal situations, such as going to the same church (76%) or to the market (72%), thus merely happening to be together at the same place. They were less comfortable with situations requiring a positive action and acceptance of members of other ethnic groups, such as sharing a drink (51 %), living in the same household (56%), or marrying with family members (47%). In all the situations, the survey reflects a striking difference among respondents in North Kivu who were, on average, markedly less comfortable with other ethnic groups compared to respondents in South Kivu and Ituri, indicating a situation where ethnic relationships are more polarized in the context of ongoing open conflict there.

TABLE 17: ATTITUDES TOWARD OTHER ETHNIC GROUPS

Percentage of respondents COMFORTABLE in the following situations in the presence of members from ANY other ethnic group?	North Kivu	South Kivu	Ituri	Total
Living in same community, village	56.3	64.1	76.1	64.2
Living as close neighbors	53.4	64.2	78.1	63.6
Living as household members	43.5	59.8	69.2	55.7
Sharing a meal	46.8	66.5	71.5	59.8
Working with them	55.4	69.8	77.3	66.0
Going to the market	62.7	72.2	85.5	72.0
Sharing a drink	40.7	57.0	59.9	51.1
Going to the same church	69.6	74.9	87.8	76.3
Marrying a family member	41.0	49.4	54.3	47.3
Going to same school as you/your children	61.2	72.4	83.5	70.9

The responses to this question are similar to those expressed for security and sense of fear, where 39 percent of respondents felt safe or very safe meeting strangers and 45 percent felt safe meeting people from another ethnic group. Nevertheless, several respondents said they had feelings of hatred toward other ethnic groups (20%) or wish they could take revenge on them (14%).

About two-thirds said that all ethnic groups from eastern Congo (64%) and Congo as a whole could live together (66%). Overall, only a few respondents answered positively to a question on whether their region should become independent (10%), most of those in Ituri (13%).

TABLE 18: UNITY

(% Strongly agree – Agree)	North Kivu	South Kivu	Ituri	Total
All ethnic groups from eastern Congo can live together	55.0	69.4	69.5	63.5
All ethnic groups from Congo can live together	59.3	71.1	71.8	66.4
This region should become independent children	8.5	7.6	13.2	9.5

Reintegration

The survey further asked respondents about their level of comfort in various situations, but this time in the presence of former combatants. (Possible affiliations of the former combatants were not discussed.) For all the situations, fewer respondents felt comfortable with former combatants compared to members of any ethnic groups. Respondents were, on average, least comfortable with having a former combatant marry a family member, share a drink (35%), or live in the same household (37%). Feelings of discomfort were expressed more frequently with regard to former combatants who committed war crimes (63%) as compared to members of any ethnic group (20%); and 22 percent said they wished they could take revenge against former combatants who committed war crimes. Generally, more respondents from Ituri felt comfortable in all these situations than those from the Kivus.

TABLE 19: ATTITUDES TOWARD FORMER COMBATANTS

Percentage of respondents COMFORTABLE in the following situations in the presence of former combatants?	North Kivu	South Kivu	Ituri	Total
Living in same community, village	26.8	44.1	63.8	42.4
Living as close neighbors	28.1	44.1	66.7	43.8
Living as household members	22.1	40.3	56.2	37.2
Sharing a meal	29.7	56.0	62.9	47.1
Working with them	33.5	54.5	68.6	49.8
Going to the market	41.4	59.2	75.5	56.4
Sharing a drink	21.6	42.3	48.1	35.4
Going to the same church	51.4	65.8	81.6	64.3
Marrying a family member	23.7	36.7	48.4	34.6
Going to same school as you/your children	44.3	61.5	78.0	59.0

In terms of the reintegration of militia leaders, the survey found that overall about one out of four respondents agreed or strongly agreed with the proposition that militia leaders have the same rights as everyone else (25%) and have the right to participate in politics and to govern if elected (27%), but these views were less shared in North Kivu. Likewise, only a minority agreed with the proposition that militia leaders should be able to participate in the national army (38%) and even fewer said those who committed war crimes could participate in the national army. In other words, respondents generally seemed to take the view that some of these rights have been forfeited by militia leaders. Again, there were regional differences, with about one in two respondents in Ituri agreeing with their participation in the national army, and only about one in four agreeing with this in the Kivus. This may reflect the more advanced stage of the "brassage" in Ituri, where this remains a difficult point in the Kivus.

TABLE 20: VETTING

(% Strongly agree – Agree)	North Kivu	South Kivu	Ituri	Total
Militia leaders have the same rights as everyone else (%)	11.7	33.3	34.9	24.8
Militia leaders have the right to participate in politics and to govern, if elected (%)	15.1	31.3	39.7	26.9
Militia leaders can be part of the national army (%)	26.7	32.3	59.9	37.6
Those who committed war crimes can be part of the national army (%)	16.6	18.9	47.7	25.9

ACCOUNTABILITY AND TRANSITIONAL JUSTICE MECHANISMS

To gauge the population's receptivity to a variety of transitional justice mechanisms, the survey asked a series of questions concerning accountability, justice, the ICC, truth-seeking processes, and reparations. Definitions of various terms were not provided to the respondents, leaving them to interpret the questions according to their own perceptions of the terms. Preliminary questions regarding views on accountability were designed to be open-ended; follow-up questions on various mechanisms for achieving accountability provided additional indications of levels of support for these approaches toward accountability.

Accountability

The survey found that accountability and justice for grave crimes are very important to most people in eastern Congo, and that people believe these concepts are linked to peace. When asked about accountability, more than four out of five respondents (85%) deemed it important to hold accountable those who committed war crimes in eastern Congo, and 82 percent believed that accountability is necessary to secure peace. When asked what crimes they thought should be made accountable, the most frequent responses were murder/killing (92%) and sexual violence (70%). These responses reflect the gravity accorded the commissions of these crimes and the clear imperative to hold accountable those who committed them. Respondents provided also a wide range of other crimes for which people must be held accountable, including burying people alive, cannibalism, and burning houses. Forced recruitment was not often mentioned: Only 6 percent of respondents mentioned forced recruitment of adults, and 22 percent mentioned forced recruitment of children (although it was the basis for the first arrest warrant by the ICC in the DRC, concerning Thomas Lubanga). Demand for accountability for displacement was more frequent in North and South Kivu than in Ituri, whereas accountability for torture was cited more often in Ituri than in the Kivus.

TABLE 21: CRIMES AND ACCOUNTABILITY

What crimes should they be held accountable for?	North Kivu	South Kivu	Ituri	Total
Murder / Killing (%)	92.5	90.2	93.4	92.0
Rape / Sexual violence (%)	73.8	66.0	68.8	69.9
Stealing cattle / livestock (%)	45.4	40.9	38.0	41.9
Displacement of populations (%)	26.6	27.0	16.9	24.1
Destruction / Looting of properties (%)	21.6	23.9	23.1	22.8
Forced recruitment of children (%)	24.3	22.6	16.5	21.6
Torture (%)	15.0	18.4	27.6	19.5
Land confiscation (%)	11.4	15.2	17.3	14.3
Forced recruitment of adults (%)	5.3	6.5	4.6	5.5
Other (%)	8.9	10.1	3.9	7.9

Respondents identified a variety of actors they believed should be held accountable, reflecting the complex involvement of numerous sources and parties in the conflicts in eastern DRC. The most frequent answers concerned militia leaders (56%) and the militias in general (44%). In some cases, respondents specified which groups should be held accountable. Respondents mentioned the Congolese government (17%) and government forces (FARDC, 13%). The demand for the government in Kinshasa to be made accountable was particularly strong in Ituri (28%) when compared with the Kivus. Respondents also recognized the role of external actors, frequently mentioning Rwanda (36%) and Uganda (23%). The role of external actors was a particular concern for those living near these countries: in North Kivu, 42 percent of respondents wanted to see Rwanda and the Rwandan government held accountable. A few mentioned MONUC and the international community should also be held accountable (2%). Only 2 percent of respondents believed no one should be held accountable.

A number of factors may explain this high demand for accountability. First, the nature of the violence, involving different social and ethnic groups, as well as foreign troops, may account for this demand to hold "the other" accountable. Second, DRC is a country where most infrastructure remains lacking, in particular in the East: a thirst for accountability may also be a thirst for judicial infrastructure, as well as more generally for law and order, and for a normalization of social relationships.

Who should be held accountable?	North Kivu	South Kivu	Ituri	Total
Militia leaders (%)	54.5	54.0	60.5	56.0
Militias (%)	44.7	42.9	43.8	43.9
Rwanda / Rwandan government (%)	42.0	35.1	29.5	36.4
Uganda / Ugandan government (%)	23.0	22.2	23.6	22.9
Government in Kinshasa (%)	12.0	15.2	27.9	17.4
National army (FARDC) (%)	12.0	14.0	12.1	12.7
The community (%)	3.4	3.8	4.0	3.7
"Those who committed violence" (%)	4.0	3.7	0.7	3.0
Police / Security agents (%)	2.4	2.3	3.0	2.6
MONUC, international community (%)	2.7	2.2	1.7	2.3
No one (%)	1.9	2.0	2.0	2.0
Ethnic group (%)	1.8	2.5	0.4	1.6
Other (%)	5.4	3.8	1.0	3.7

When asked who or which institutions should hold people accountable, respondents most frequently saw this as the role of the government (80%). The national judicial system was mentioned by less than a quarter of respondents (22%), illustrating a possible lack of trust in this system, as well as misunderstanding of the respective role and nature of the government and of the judiciary. The ICC was considered a relevant mechanism of accountability by almost a quarter of the respondents (24%). About one out of five respondents also saw a role for the international community (22%). Traditional justice mechanisms were cited by only a few respondents as means of holding people accountable: 6 percent would entrust this to customary/traditional leaders, and only 3 percent to religious leaders. The reliance on customary/traditional leaders to hold those responsible accountable was higher in Ituri (13%) than in the Kivus. Only 2 percent of respondents would rely on an amnesty process, reiterating their attachment to accountability.

Who should hold them accountable?	North Kivu	South Kivu	Ituri	Total
Government (%)	78.8	79.9	82.4	80.1
International Criminal Court (%)	21.8	24.7	28.0	24.4
National judicial system (%)	22.1	20.1	24.9	22.2
International community (%)	22.2	20.1	22.3	21.6
Customary/Traditional leaders (%)	3.7	3.4	13.2	6.2
Representatives of ethnic groups (%)	3.7	2.8	6.2	4.1
Religious leaders (%)	3.9	3.2	2.6	3.3
Amnesty process (%)	2.3	1.2	3.9	2.4
God (%)	2.5	1.6	0.9	1.8
Other (%)	4.7	4.0	3.3	4.1

The survey then asked respondents what they would like to see happen to those who committed war crimes (the term "war crimes" was not explained, see Table 24). A large majority of respondents supported sanctions and punishments: 69 percent of respondents said war criminals should be punished, 34 percent said that war criminals should be put in jail, and 20 percent felt war criminals should be killed. Having those responsible confess their crimes was mentioned by only 8 percent of respondents; even fewer respondents said war criminals should be forgiven (7%) or reintegrated in the community (5%). Overall, 23 percent mentioned forgiveness and reintegration.[33]

The survey also asked respondents if they believed foot soldiers should be treated in the same way as leaders. One-third (38%) of respondents said they should be treated similarly, indicating that the vast majority of respondents believe that leaders bear greater responsibility for the commission of war crimes than foot soldiers.

33. In comparison, using a similar question in northern Uganda, we found that 42.5% of the respondents were willing to forgive LRA leaders. However, the type and origins of the conflicts differ in many respects, including the fact that in Uganda many of the perpetrators and victims come from the same social group, the Acholi. Pham PN, et al., "When the War Ends: A Population-Based Survey on Attitudes about Peace, Justice, and Social Reconstruction in Northern Uganda," Human Rights Center, University of California, Berkeley; Payson Center for International Development, Tulane University; International Center for Transitional Justice, New York (December 2007).

What would you like to see happen to those who committed war crimes?	North Kivu	South Kivu	Ituri	Total
Punish them (%)	71.0	68.5	66.5	68.9
Put them in jail (%)	33.2	32.9	35.8	33.8
See them in trials/court (%)	24.4	19.3	33.8	25.3
Kill them (%)	19.4	20.0	19.5	19.6
Have them compensate victims (%)	16.6	17.3	18.4	17.3
They should ask for forgiveness (%)	7.9	9.7	10.8	9.3
They should confess their crimes (%)	8.8	9.0	5.5	7.9
Demobilize them (%)	8.8	7.4	7.1	7.9
They should be forgiven (%)	6.1	7.0	8.7	7.1
Give them amnesty (%)	3.9	5.0	9.0	5.7
Reintegrate them in the community (%)	2.7	4.0	8.2	4.6
They should go back to their country (%)	3.3	3.1	0.7	2.5
Other (%)	2.8	2.8	1.4	2.4

Justice

Before asking specific questions about justice mechanisms, the survey asked respondents what, in their opinion, is the meaning of justice. Establishing the truth (51%), being just or fair (48%), and applying the law (49%) were cited most frequently and almost equally. These responses suggest that justice is primarily viewed in relation to judicial mechanisms and the rule of law. This may be viewed as paradoxical given the absence of fully functioning justice institutions in eastern Congo and shows an appetite for such institutions. Support for applying the law drew the highest support in Ituri, where the stabilization of conflict has allowed for efforts to reform the judicial sector there at a faster pace than elsewhere in eastern DRC. The results of the survey on this point lend support to the positive impact that international efforts at judicial sector reform can have in increasing the Congolese population's faith in the rule of law.

Punishment itself is perceived as constituting justice for more respondents (21%) than trials are (14%). This insistence on punishment underlines an understanding of justice as being predominantly retributive. This was confirmed by the fact that apologies and forgiveness were only mentioned by a few (3%).

As for obtaining compensation for the victims, it was perceived as constituting justice by only 8 percent of the respondents. This is in contrast to the number of respondents (17%) that would like war criminals to compensate victims (see attitudes towards war criminals). Again, this low correlation of compensation constituting justice could be a reflection that thus far, the Congolese justice system has been ineffective at concluding trials, attributing guilt, and ordering compensation.

In your opinion, what is the meaning of "justice"?	North Kivu	South Kivu	Ituri	Total
Establish the truth (%)	48.9	54.1	49.9	50.8
Apply the law (%)	43.6	49.4	54.8	48.5
To be just/fair (%)	47.9	44.3	51.1	47.6
Punish those responsible (%)	22.7	20.4	20.5	21.4
A trial for those responsible (%)	13.3	11.1	19.7	14.3
Compensate the victims (%)	7.8	6.8	9.7	8.0
Those responsible acknowledge their crimes (%)	3.4	2.8	4.5	3.5
Forgive those who committed crimes (%)	2.7	2.5	5.5	3.4
Those responsible apologize (%)	2.4	2.0	4.2	2.8
Those responsible ask for forgiveness (%)	1.5	2.6	5.1	2.8
Peace (%)	1.1	2.1	0.7	1.3
Other (%)	6.7	4.6	3.9	5.2
Don't know (%)	2.2	1.5	0.9	1.6

The survey then asked respondents whether it is possible to achieve justice and what means should be used to achieve it. Most respondents were optimistic and believed justice can indeed be achieved (80%). As for the means to achieve justice, consistent with their perception of justice as being predominantly retributive, over half the respondents mentioned the national court system (51%), a quarter referred to the ICC (26%), and a fifth to military courts (20%). Non-adjudicatory alternatives mentioned included a truth mechanism (20%), and conflict-resolution projects initiated by NGOs and religious groups (14%). Traditional or customary mechanisms were mentioned by 15 percent of respondents. Amnesty and forgiveness were cited by only 7 percent of respondents, reflecting respondents' prevalent perception of justice as official mechanisms that apply the law and establish the truth in an equitable manner. Support for the national court system and the ICC as means to achieve justice was highest in Ituri, where efforts to reform the judicial sector and ICC investigations are further advanced than in North and South Kivu.

What means must be used to have justice?	North Kivu	South Kivu	Ituri	Total
National court system (%)	47.2	46.0	61.2	50.6
International Criminal Court (%)	22.1	23.3	33.3	25.6
Military court (%)	21.2	18.5	21.2	20.3
Truth mechanism (%)	17.2	21.0	23.7	20.2
Traditional (customary) justice (%)	12.0	13.5	22.8	15.4
Put them in jail (%)	16.1	14.8	14.1	15.1
Conflict-resolution projects (NGOs, religious organizations) (%)	16.1	15.4	10.5	14.3
Grant amnesty, forgive (%)	6.4	4.7	9.2	6.6
Dialogue, unity (%)	4.1	3.7	1.9	3.4
God (%)	3.3	2.5	3.1	3.0
No means, nothing can be done (%)	2.4	3.6	2.2	2.7
Revenge (%)	3.1	1.6	3.2	2.6
Don't know (%)	2.3	1.5	0.9	1.7
Other means for justice (%)	16.0	18.5	5.1	13.8

Most respondents favored peace with trials (62%) over peace with amnesty (38%). This confirms the support for judicial accountability and retribution highlighted by other parts of the survey. The survey then asked respondents to choose between various trial options: 45 percent chose national trials, 40 percent chose international trials in DRC, 7 percent chose international trials abroad, and only 8 percent chose no trials at all.

Most significantly, the results suggest that 85 percent of respondents wanted trials held in DRC, whether they are national (45%) or internationalized trials in the DRC (40%). Furthermore, respondents expressed a preference for trials with international oversight, whether internationalized trials in DRC (40%) or international trials abroad (7%). Considering the option of national trials, most respondents (82%) said the international community should help the domestic courts.

	North Kivu	South Kivu	Ituri	Total
Would you forgive war criminals if it is the only way to have peace? (% yes)	67.1	72.5	65.2	68.3
Would you forgive those who directly attacked you if it was the only way to have peace? (% yes)	67.5	70.8	64.0	67.6
Two choices — Peace with trials (%)	60.9	57.7	68.3	61.9
or Peace with forgiveness (%)	39.1	42.3	31.7	38.1
Four choices — National trials (%)	48.4	42.5	41.6	44.7
or International trials in DRC (%)	37.4	39.2	44.6	39.9
or International trials abroad (%)	6.1	7.3	9.0	7.3
or No trials (%)	8.1	8.1	4.8	8.1
Should the international community help local courts? (% yes)	81.3	81.3	80.8	81.9

THE INTERNATIONAL CRIMINAL COURT

Only a quarter of the respondents had heard of the ICC (27%) or the proceedings against Thomas Lubanga (28%). Surprisingly, respondents in Ituri were no more familiar with the Lubanga proceedings or the ICC than those in North and South Kivu, although, to date, ICC arrest warrants in the DRC were only for crimes allegedly committed in Ituri. When asked how they heard about the ICC, 85 percent of respondents identified the radio or television as their source of information. Among those who had heard about the ICC, 16 percent also said they had heard about the ICC's Trust Fund for Victims. A majority of those interviewed would like to participate in ICC activities (67%), but only 12 percent knew how to access the International Criminal Court, showing a need for more information from and about the ICC.

TABLE 28: KNOWLEDGE OF THE ICC

	North Kivu	South Kivu	Ituri	Total
Have you heard about the Lubanga proceeding? (% yes)	27.8	27.5	29.3	28.1
Have you heard about the ICC? (% yes)	25.7	27.6	26.9	26.6
(If heard about the ICC) Did you hear about the Trust Fund for Victims at the ICC? (% yes)	15.6	13.0	18.6	15.6
Do you know how to access the ICC? (% yes)	14.4	10.3	10.8	12.1
Would you like to participate in ICC activities? (% yes)	66.5	67.1	68.2	67.2

The survey asked respondents who had heard about the Lubanga proceedings what they thought about it. Respondents said that "it was good" (35%) or that Lubanga should be punished (34%). Considerably fewer said that "it was not good" (13%) or that he should be forgiven (2%). Some respondents said that others should be tried (7%). Only 3 percent responded that the Lubanga trial should be held in the DRC; this conflicts with other survey responses indicating a strong preference among the respondents for trials in the DRC. This could be a result of a lack of awareness that the ICC could potentially hold *in situ* trials in the DRC.

The survey further asked a series of questions to those who had heard about the ICC. Over three-quarters believed it had the power to arrest suspected criminals (77%), the belief being strongest in Ituri (84%).[34] Perceptions of a lack of neutrality or impartiality are an issue for the ICC. Nearly one-third (28%) of respondents believed the ICC was not neutral because it did not do anything to help (27%), worked with the government (24%), was only after one ethnic group (14%), or did not arrest the criminals (12%). Again, this illustrates a need for more information and outreach to be conducted by and on the ICC in the DRC.

Truth-Seeking

Respondents in eastern Congo valued truth-seeking as an important feature of moving forward: 88 percent considers it important to know the truth about what happened. When asked how the truth could be established, over half the respondents mentioned an inquiry by the judicial system, showing again a preference for and faith in official structures of judiciary mechanisms for attaining the truth. The rate of support for inquiries by the judicial system was highest in Ituri, which has experienced the greatest progress in local reform of its judicial sector, compared to the Kivus.

A truth commission was mentioned by only 24 percent of respondents in eastern DRC. This result must be viewed against the experience during the Congolese transition of the creation of an official Congolese Truth and Reconciliation Commission, as pursuant to a resolution undertaken with the Sun City peace accords in 2002. That Commission, however, failed to conduct any serious activities. The low support for truth commissions expressed in the survey could reflect either a lack of awareness or understanding of the option of truth commissions, or a lack of faith in truth commissions because of the experience of the one that transpired during the transition as a politicized and ineffective mechanism.

---

34. The ICC does not have the power to carry out arrests by itself and relies on cooperation by states and regional or international organizations to accomplish this.

	North Kivu	South Kivu	Ituri	Total
Is it important to know the truth about what happened in eastern Congo? (% yes)	87.8	88.3	88.4	88.1
How can the truth be established?				
Inquiry by judicial system (%)	50.6	55.3	65.1	56.1
Let people talk freely (%)	28.3	29.3	39.2	31.6
Have a truth / inquiry commission (%)	22.0	23.6	28.6	24.3
Independent, free media (%)	23.8	23.7	25.3	24.2
Write a book (%)	13.7	11.8	9.0	11.8
Dialogue, reconciliation (%)	1.4	1.1	0.6	1.1
Don't know (%)	2.2	2.0	1.2	1.9
Other (%)	10.8	11.4	4.8	9.4

Although the population recognizes the general importance of truth-seeking exercises and aspires to know to the truth, security remains a significant barrier to talking openly about what has happened in eastern Congo. Only about two out of three respondents (63%) said they would agree to talk openly about what happened to them or their families.[35] Those who would not agree to do so most frequently cited fear of revenge or retaliation (50%). Fear of talking openly about the conflict was also examined when exploring the sense of safety among respondents (see Security): only one out of three respondents (30%) said they would feel safe or very safe talking openly about what they experienced during the conflict. Other respondents indicated that talking about what happened would be useless (23%) or that they have nothing to say (21%). The feeling of uselessness was more intense in Ituri (33%) than in the Kivus.

35. In comparison, 89 percent of the respondents were willing to talk openly about their experience during the conflict in northern Uganda according to our 2007 survey. Pham PN, et al., "When the War Ends: A Population-Based Survey on Attitudes about Peace, Justice, and Social Reconstruction in Northern Uganda," Human Rights Center, University of California, Berkeley; Payson Center for International Development, Tulane University; International Center for Transitional Justice, New York (December 2007).

	North Kivu	South Kivu	Ituri	Total
Have you participated in a process to establish the truth? (% yes)	24.3	24.2	23.7	24.1
Would you be willing to talk openly about what happened to you or your family? (% yes)	59.3	59.9	69.7	62.5
If not, why not?				
I have nothing to say (%)	20.2	20.5	24.3	21.2
It is useless (%)	24.0	14.8	32.9	23.0
Fear of revenge, retaliation (%)	48.2	59.7	40.0	50.1
No freedom of expression (%)	1.3	1.3	0.5	1.1
Other (%)	5.6	3.4	1.4	3.9
Don't know (%)	0.8	0.3	1.0	0.7

Reparations and Memorialization

The survey then asked respondents "what, if anything," should be done for the victims. This question was asked without reference to achieving accountability or justice for the victims, and the respondents therefore revealed a wide range of material needs it believed would serve as a form of non-judicial compensation for their suffering. The most frequent answers focused on providing victims with material compensation, including money (40%), housing (28%), food (28%), and other material compensation (40%). Most respondents said such reparations should be provided to both individuals and the community as a whole (43%); 35 percent said it should be for individuals only, and 22 percent for the community only. One out of five considered that punishing those responsible should be done for the victims, and 17 percent indicated that an official recognition of the victims' suffering would also be important. Psychological counseling was only mentioned by 15 percent of respondents overall, but by 20 percent of the respondents in Ituri. This must be assessed against a background of quasi-nonexistence of formal psychological counseling in eastern DRC, and stresses the need for more to be made available to the victims.

What should be done for victims?	North Kivu	South Kivu	Ituri	Total
Receive money (%)	35.5	38.2	47.6	39.7
Other material compensation (%)	42.7	44.6	28.9	39.5
Receive housing (%)	25.1	24.6	37.2	28.3
Receive food (%)	26.6	24.8	34.0	28.1
Receive health care (%)	21.4	29.1	26.7	25.2
Punish those responsible (%)	16.0	22.4	20.9	19.4
Go to school, support for education (%)	14.8	15.0	23.7	17.3
Official recognition of their suffering (%)	16.5	18.3	15.8	16.9
Psychological counseling (%)	12.5	13.4	20.6	15.0
Receive apologies (%)	14.5	14.9	15.4	14.8
Receive cattle, livestock (%)	9.5	11.1	13.3	11.0
Receive land (%)	8.8	10.3	14.2	10.8
Peace, security (%)	4.8	4.2	0.4	3.4
Nothing (%)	3.6	3.1	2.8	3.2
Aid, assistance, unspecified (%)	2.5	3.0	2.4	2.6
Other (%)	5.1	4.7	1.9	4.1

A majority of respondents (60%) said reparations should be paid by the Congolese government. As this question was asked separately from questions regarding justice and accountability, the responses to this question indicate an overall reliance on the structures of the State and the government for providing various services. Only 21 percent said reparations should be paid by those who committed the violence and 11 percent saw it as the duty of the international community. Although survey respondents indicated an expectation of the international community to provide development assistance to satisfy livelihood concerns more broadly (see Figure 4), respondents do not hold the international community accountable for paying reparations for suffering caused by local belligerents (11%).

TABLE 32: PAYMENT OF REPARATIONS

Who should pay for the reparations?	North Kivu	South Kivu	Ituri	Total
Those who committed the violence (%)	19.2	21.7	22.7	20.9
The community / population (%)	0.8	1.4	1.8	1.3
The Congolese government (%)	60.9	59.5	57.7	59.6
The international community (%)	10.1	9.9	13.4	10.9
Other (%)	9.0	7.6	4.5	7.3

About half the respondents (52%) answered positively when asked if some sort of memorial should be established to address what happened in eastern Congo. Those who said yes most frequently proposed to establish a day of remembrance (45%) or a physical object or monument (31%).

TABLE 33: MEMORIALS

What sort of memorial should be established?	North Kivu	South Kivu	Ituri	Total
An object, monument, physical piece (%)	27.2	29.8	37.3	30.7
Day of remembrance (%)	43.7	50.2	42.0	45.4
Books, written documents (%)	16.4	11.3	11.5	13.5
Films, movies (%)	10.0	7.6	11.0	9.4
Infrastructure (%)	2.8	2.5	1.8	2.5
Other (%)	5.5	4.6	1.6	4.2
Don't know (%)	3.3	3.4	0.5	2.6

MEDIA ACCESS TO INFORMATION

Access to information is critical in shaping views and opinions on issues such as peace and justice. Most respondents felt they were little or not at all informed about the situation in eastern Congo (not at all: 18%; a little: 43%) and even fewer felt informed about justice in general (not at all: 32%; a little: 43%).

Radio programs were the primary source of information about what happens in the community for two-thirds of respondents (67%), followed by friends, family and the community in general (23%). More than half the respondents (54%) listened to the radio on a daily basis while 17 percent never listened to it. In comparison, only 4 percent of respondents read newspapers on a daily basis while two-thirds (66%) never read one. The main programs respondents listened to on the radio were the news (49%) and political programs (15%). Respondents generally trusted radio programs (more so than newspapers). Nevertheless, about half the respondents believed that journalists were only a little (31%) or not at all free (20%) to report on social and political issues.

	Not at All	A Little	Moderately	A Lot	Extremely	Don't Know
Do you feel informed about situation in eastern DRC? (%)	18.1	42.9	22.0	14.2	2.8	--
Do you feel informed about justice in general? (%)	31.7	43.2	17.6	6.9	0.5	--
Are journalists free to report openly on social and political issues? (%)	19.7	30.9	23.6	16.2	2.5	7.0
Do you trust newspapers? (%)	31.8	28.6	16.4	7.5	1.1	14.6
Do you trust the radio? (%)	9.4	28.8	26.6	26.0	4.9	4.3

COMPARATIVE SURVEY RESULTS FROM KINSHASA AND KISANGANI

This section compares and contrasts the findings of the survey results from eastern Congo with the survey results from Kinshasa and Kisangani. The objective of the survey was to gauge attitudes and perceptions of the populations of eastern DRC most affected by ongoing conflict. As such, 2,620 interviews were conducted throughout the Ituri district of Oriental province and the provinces of North and South Kivu. An additional 1,133 surveys were conducted in Kinshasa (592) and Kisangani (541) as points of comparison with the results from eastern DRC. As Congo's capital and seat of national government, Kinshasa is far removed from the realities of the ongoing conflicts in eastern DRC. The survey reveals that there are clear divergences of views and perceptions between Kinshasa and eastern DRC. For its part, Kisangani, as described in the background section on the Congo conflicts, experienced intense fighting during the Second Congo War, but fighting subsided for the most part during the transition. The survey reveals that Kisangani's mixed history of prior intense suffering as a result of armed conflict and relatively recent peace results in some shared attitudes and perceptions with Kinshasa on the one hand and eastern DRC on the other.

As was the case in eastern DRC, the sample was selected regardless of any selection criteria with the exception of age (only adults aged 18 or older were interviewed). Same-sex interviews were also conducted here (i.e., women interviewed women and men interviewed men). In Kinshasa, the sample comprises about 100 ethnic groups, with seven groups accounting for 53 percent of respondents: Kongo (14%), Luba (11%), Mbala (8%), Yaka (6%), Yombe (5%), Yansi (5%) and Nyanga (5%). In Kisangani, about 80 ethnic groups were represented in the sample, with four groups each representing 5 percent or more of the sample and accounting for 46 percent of the total sample: Lokele (21%), Poke (12%), Mbole (7%), Kusu (6%), Yombe (5%), Yansi (5%) and Nyanga (5%). The fifth largest group was the Kusu (4%). In total those five groups represented over 50 percent of the sample. Table 35 provides detail of the main ethnic groups by zone under study.

The mean age of respondents was 32.6 years old (S.D. 11.98) in Kinshasa and 34.8 years old (S.D. 13.53) in Kisangani. In Kinshasa, about half the respondents described themselves as single and never married (49%) or as married or in a marital relationship (41%). In Kisangani, respondents were more frequently married or in a marital relationship (66%) while only 24 percent were single, never married. The average household size was 7.5 (S.D. 3.42) in Kinshasa and 9.5 (S.D. 5.25) in Kisangani. Most respondents lived in households that had children (Kinshasa: 81%, Kisangani: 91%). Looking at religion, most respondents described themselves as Catholic (Kinshasa: 28%, Kisangani: 33%) or Protestant (21% and 24% respectively). In Kinshasa, one quarter of the respondents (28%) adhered to 'Eglise du Reveil,' a form of evangelical Christianity (3% in Kisangani and 1% in eastern DRC).

TABLE 35: SOCIODEMOGRAPHIC CHARACTERISTICS OF RESPONDENTS IN KINSHASA AND KISANGANI

	Kinshasa		Kisangani
Sample size (n)	592	Sample size (n)	541
Gender (% female)	49.7	Gender (% female)	51.4
Mean Age (S.D.)		Mean Age (S.D.)	
Ethnicity*		Ethnicity*	
Kongo (%)	14.3	Lokele (%)	21.2
Luba (%)	10.8	Poke (%)	11.8
Mbala (%)	7.6	Mbole (%)	6.8
Yaka (%)	5.9	Kusu (%)	5.9
Yombe (%)	5.1	Kumu (%)	4.4
Yansi (%)	4.9		
Nyanga (%)	4.7		

* Ethnic groups are provided by order of importance. Only groups that represented about 5% or more of the respondents are provided.

Not unexpectedly, *exposure to violence* was lower in Kinshasa and Kisangani compared to the East. Nevertheless, even in those cities, respondents frequently reported experiencing traumatic events. For example, in Kinshasa, 41 percent of respondents reported having been displaced at some point since 1993, and 25 percent said they had been beaten by armed groups, compared to 81 percent and 46 percent respectively in eastern Congo. Still, 65 percent of respondents in Kinshasa and 61 percent of those in Kisangani identified themselves as victims of the conflicts, compared to 81 percent of those in eastern Congo. Four percent of respondents in Kinshasa reported having experienced sexual violence as part of the conflict, compared to as many as 16 percent in eastern Congo.

Different priorities: Fifty-seven percent of respondents in Kinshasa and 47 percent in Kisangani identified the economy or employment as one of their priorities, compared to 15 percent in the East. Respondents in Kinshasa and Kisangani also more frequently identified food and education as priorities compared to those in the East. By contrast, respondents identified security as a priority more frequently in the East (34%) compared to Kisangani (22%) and Kinshasa (5%). Peace was identified as a priority more frequently in both the East (51%) and Kisangani (56%) than in Kinshasa (32%). These results were reflected in the priorities respondents identified for the government.

The different priorities result from the fact that there is continuing open armed conflict in eastern DRC while the violence and fear wrought by the absence of security is not felt in Kinshasa and Kisangani. In the absence of violence, respondents in Kinshasa and Kisangani express the acute need for improvement of their economic situation and quality of life. This suggests that some efforts at raising awareness at the national level should occur. To the extent that ongoing conflict in eastern DRC threatens to destabilize the fragile state structure, raising the specter of renewed violence that would affect the entire country, Kinshasa and the rest of the DRC should develop solidarity with the suffering populations of the East and commit to end violence there.

Respondents were also asked what the priorities of the international community should be, to which respondents in Kinshasa and Kisangani identified peace (47% and 24% respectively) and security (22% and 20% respectively) more frequently than those in the East (peace: 24%, security: 19%). This may result from a different exposure to the international community in the different regions. For one, Kinshasa is exposed to various entities of the international community, including international development actors, UN entities, bilateral and multilateral actors. Furthermore, MONUC is highly visible in Kinshasa, albeit in the form of its headquarters as a political, diplomatic, and administrative actor. As such, the Kinshasa population is likely to be aware of MONUC's mandate without engaging on a day–to–day level with MONUC as peacekeeping troops and therefore holds a different perspective on what MONUC can achieve.

Respondents in Kinshasa and Kisangani, on average, ranked their level of *security* better than those in eastern Congo, especially in social situations such as meeting strangers and meeting people from another ethnic group. This is also reflected in the higher average *level of comfort* in a range of situations when in the presence of a member from any other ethnic group. In Kinshasa, over 90 percent of respondents felt comfortable living in the same community (90%), sharing a meal (93%) or working (93%) with a member of any other ethnic group, compared to two-thirds or less in eastern Congo (living in the same community: 64%; sharing a meal: 60%; working together: 66%). The levels of comfort for this range of situation in Kisangani were similar to the levels in eastern Congo. Looking at the same range of situations, but this time in the presence of *former combatants*, the levels of comfort in Kinshasa and Kisangani were, on average, similar or even lower than those in eastern Congo.

Respondents in Kinshasa, Kisangani, and eastern Congo defined *peace* in similar terms. They also saw it predominantly as the role of the government to bring peace. However, respondents in Kinshasa proposed more frequently (33%) that dialogue with the militias was needed to achieve peace compared to those in Kisangani (27%) and eastern Congo (22%). Respondents in Kinshasa were also more frequently convinced that the stakeholders were committed to achieving peace (76%) compared to Kisangani (54%) and eastern Congo (58%).

Respondents in all regions believed it is important to hold *accountable* those who committed crimes in eastern Congo, and views differed little regarding which crimes they should be held accountable for. Respondents in eastern Congo put an emphasis less frequently on holding the government accountable (17%) compared to those in Kinshasa (32%) and Kisangani (35%), but they more frequently identified Rwanda and Rwandan groups among those that should be held accountable. Overall, the results from Kinshasa, Kisangani, and eastern DRC as displayed in the table below reveal similar awareness and desire to hold accountable the various parties to the conflicts in the Congo, namely militia leaders, militias, Rwanda, Uganda, and the Congolese government.

TABLE 36: WHO SHOULD BE HELD ACCOUNTABLE?

Who should be held accountable?	Kinshasa	Kisangani	Eastern Congo	Total
No one (%)	1.7	1.7	2.0	1.9
Militia leaders (%)	51.4	51.6	56.0	54.6
Militias (%)	43.2	38.6	43.9	43.0
Rwanda / Rwandan government (%)	24.3	34.6	36.4	34.2
Uganda / Uganda government (%)	24.7	25.5	22.9	23.6
Government in Kinshasa (%)	31.6	35.3	17.4	22.3
National Army (FARDC) (%)	12.0	15.0	12.7	12.9
The community (%)	4.2	4.6	3.7	3.9
Police / Security agents (%)	2.9	4.1	2.6	2.8
MONUC, international community (%)	2.5	3.0	2.3	2.4
"Those who committed violence" (%)	1.4	0.9	3.0	2.4
Ethnic group (%)	0.2	0.4	1.6	1.2
Other (%)	1.5	2.8	3.7	3.2

When asked directly what should happen to those who committed crimes, about two-thirds of respondents in Kinshasa, Kisangani, and eastern DRC said they should be punished. Respondents in Kinshasa and Kisangani also said more frequently they wanted to see them in court (Kinshasa: 41%; Kisangani: 39%; eastern Congo: 25%).

Despite the different ways Kinshasa, Kisangani, and eastern Congo have experienced the Congo conflicts, views and attitudes towards justice, transitional mechanisms, the ICC, and truth-seeking mechanisms differed little across regions. One exception was that, among the trial options (national courts, international court in Congo, International Court abroad, or no trial), respondents in Kinshasa chose more frequently an international court abroad (20%) compared to those in Kisangani (9%) and eastern Congo (7%). The other respondents were about evenly divided between national courts and an international court in Congo. Overall, few chose no trials at all (5% each in Kinshasa and Kisangani, 8% in eastern Congo). Because access to media is higher in Kinshasa compared to the interior, 34 percent of respondents had heard of the Lubanga proceedings in Kinshasa compared to 30 percent in Kisangani and 28 percent in eastern Congo. More respondents in Kinshasa said they had heard of the ICC (39%) than in Kisangani (25%) and in eastern Congo (27%). The greater awareness of the ICC in

Kinshasa likely influences the survey finding that 20 percent of respondents in Kinshasa favor international trials abroad to hold war criminals accountable.

TABLE 37: GENERAL COMPARISON: KNOWLEDGE OF ICC

	Kinshasa	Kisangani	Eastern Congo	Total
Have you heard about the Lubanga trial? (% yes)	34.3	30.3	28.1	29.4
Have you heard about the ICC? (% yes)	38.5	25.3	26.6	28.3

With regard to truth-seeking, the main mechanism advanced to establish the truth was an inquiry by the judicial system, proposed by over half the respondents in all three regions. Respondents in Kinshasa and Kisangani also more frequently proposed a form of truth-seeking commission (Kinshasa: 35%, Kisangani: 36%) compared to those in eastern Congo (24%). This could be because respondents in Kinshasa and Kisangani received greater information about the official Truth and Reconciliation Commission sponsored by the transitional Congolese government.

Finally, respondents in Kinshasa and Kisangani were more receptive to the idea of talking openly about their experience in the conflict (73% and 75% respectively) as compared to those in eastern Congo (63%), possibly reflecting the higher level of security and also anonymity in the two urban settings.

CONCLUSIONS AND RECOMMENDATIONS

SUMMARY FINDINGS

Survey Results from Eastern DRC

The population of eastern DRC has been exposed to a high prevalence of violence and suffered serious and widespread human rights abuses and violations of international humanitarian law perpetrated by belligerents in Congo's previous and current conflicts. There is abundant evidence of the warring parties attacking villages, markets, churches, and hospitals, and other structures necessary for the survival and welfare of civilians.[36] Formal and informal armed groups and militias also routinely steal cattle and destroy fields necessary for people's survival. While the extent of the violence remains to be fully examined and documented, the present survey of eastern Congo revealed:

- A majority of the population surveyed in eastern Congo experienced having one or more household members disappear (60%), were interrogated or persecuted by armed groups (55%), forced to work or enslaved (53%), were beaten by armed groups (46%) or threatened with death (46%), or were themselves abducted for at least a week (34%).

- Most respondents experienced the violent death of a family member or friend (61%) or a household member (42%); most families also suffered deaths due to disease or malnutrition (56%).

- Most respondents reported being displaced at least once (81%), while the average respondent had been displaced approximately three times. Twenty percent of respondents remained displaced at the time of the survey with the largest displaced population (33%) in North Kivu.

- Among respondents in eastern Congo, 16 percent were victims of sexual violence and 23 percent witnessed an act of sexual violence. One-third of the respondents said they would not accept victims of sexual violence back in their community.

---

36. Van Herp M, Parque V, Rackley E, Ford N, "Mortality, Violence and Lack of Access to Health Care in the Democratic Republic of Congo," *Disasters* 27/2 (2003): 141–153.

- More than two-thirds of respondents (66% to 87%) indicated that they lacked food/water, health care, housing, and had their homes or property destroyed or confiscated during the conflicts.

The widespread commission of crimes means that Congolese civilians have learned to flee their homes at the first signs of violence; but this forced flight itself undermines the traditional survival strategies of rural populations and weakens their community. Wage earners are often the first to be killed; armed groups then target survivors and the younger members of the community for forced recruitment. In an environment where State services and administration, are already minimal, the disruption of civilian livelihoods is compounded by little or no access to medical, psychological, and other social services. As a result of these man-made, interrelated calamities, malnutrition and infant mortality are driven to extremes, and many of the healthy easily succumb to preventable and curable diseases.

Respondents identified several factors contributing to the *origins of the conflicts* in a variety of complex and interlinked causes. The most frequently cited factors were power or politics (47%), the exploitation of natural resources (37%), land issues (35%), and ethnic divisions (29%). Responses in North Kivu and South Kivu were comparable. In Ituri, however, 60 percent of respondents identified conflicts over land as the primary catalyst for collective violence, while conflicts over power, ethnic divisions, and natural resources were less frequently identified. In the three regions, respondents mentioned problems of nationality (15%) and the relationship with Rwanda (5%), including the influx of refugees after the 1994 genocide, and Rwandan support for rebel groups, as factors contributing to the violence.

The population in eastern Congo continues to live in fear of violence, even while conducting the most basic daily tasks, and feels the least secure when they encounter soldiers or armed groups.

- Respondents felt least safe when meeting soldiers or armed groups, but also when talking openly about their experiences, walking at night in their villages, or meeting strangers.

- A third (38%) believed that the recomposed National Congolese Army (FARDC) protected them. Respondents also felt that no one (6%) or "only God" (31%) protected them.

- Most respondents described their lives in general as the same (42%) or worse (39%) now compared to before the 2002 peace agreement and the same (51%) or worse (39%) than before the 2006 presidential elections.

In this context, it is not surprising that respondents' priorities in eastern DRC are peace and security:

- A majority of respondents indicated peace as their first priority (51%) and security as the second highest priority (34%).

- After peace and security, respondents cited social concerns, such as money (27%), education (26%), and food and water (26%).

- For the respondents, the Congolese government's top priorities should include peace (51%) and providing security (42%).

- By contrast, respondents most frequently indicated that development should be the international community's top priority (36%), followed by financial aid/money (28%), and the provision of food and water (23%).

- Justice was seldom mentioned among respondents' own priorities and more frequently among what they felt should be the government and international community priorities.

A strong majority of respondents in eastern Congo believed that peace could be achieved (90%). Most defined peace as the ability to live together, united and reconciled (49%), the absence of fear (47%) and of violence (41%).

- The vast majority of respondents believed the Congolese government could bring durable peace to eastern Congo (86%).

- Respondents endorsed a multifaceted understanding of what is require to achieve peace, including arrest of those responsible for crimes (28%), dialogue between ethnic groups (22%), dialogue with the militias (22%), establishing the truth (20%), and a military victory over the armed groups (17%).

An overwhelming majority of respondents surveyed in eastern Congo believed accountability is necessary to achieve peace (82%), with four out of five respondents (85%) affirming the importance of holding those who committed grave crimes accountable.

- Most respondents believe that among those who should be held accountable are militia leaders (56%), militias more generally (44%), Rwanda or the Rwandan government (36%), Uganda or the Ugandan government (23%), the Congolese government (17%) and the Congolese National Army (13%).

- Most respondents wanted to see those who committed grave crimes punished (69%), put in jail (34%), or tried by a court of justice (25%). Few respondents supported forgiving perpetrators of these crimes (7%) or giving them amnesty (6%).

Importantly, despite the general impunity that has prevailed so far, most respondents in eastern Congo still believe that justice can be achieved (80%).

- Respondents defined justice according to several rule-of-law attributes, including establishing the truth (51%), applying the law (49%), being just/fair (48%), punishing those responsible (21%), and holding trials for those suspected of committing crimes (14%).

- The means to achieve justice cited most frequently by respondents are: the national justice system (51%), the ICC (26%), military courts (20%), a truth-seeking mechanism (20%), traditional (customary) justice (15%), or other conflict-resolution mechanisms (14%).

Respondents showed support for prosecutions, with a distinct preference for trials held in-country, whether national or internationalized.

- Respondents from eastern Congo expressed a strong preference for obtaining both peace and justice (62%) over a peace based on amnesty (38%).

- One-third of respondents were unwilling to forgive, even if it were the only way to achieve peace. But a majority (68%) would accept or forgive criminals if doing so were the only way to attain peace, even if perpetrators had directly attacked them. This suggests that given the choice, respondents favor accountability and trials, but their priority is to achieve peace.

- Presented with various trial options, 45 percent of respondents chose trials conducted by the domestic judicial system, 40 percent chose trials conducted by an international jurisdiction but in Congo, 7 percent chose international trials abroad, and 8 percent chose no trials at all. In sum, 85 percent of respondents wanted trials held in DRC, whether national or international, and respondents expressed a preference for trials with international oversight (47%), whether in DRC or abroad, over domestic trials (45%).

Approximately one-quarter of respondents in eastern Congo had heard of the ICC (27%) or of its proceedings against the first Congolese to appear before this Court, Thomas Lubanga Dyilo (28%).

- Among those who had heard about the ICC, a majority held the false view that the Court itself could arrest criminals (77%).

- Some of the respondents in eastern Congo believe the ICC is not neutral (28%), most frequently because they saw it as doing nothing to help (27%), working with the government (24%), investigating only one (ethnic) group (14%), or not arresting criminals (12%).

A strong majority of respondents surveyed in eastern Congo (88%) affirmed the importance of truth-seeking.

- When asked how truth could be established, over half of the respondents identified the national judicial system (56%), showing again their primary reliance on this system. A third of respondents believed that the truth can be established by allowing people to talk freely (32%). Only a quarter refers to obtaining truth through a truth commission (24%) or an independent and free media (24%).

- Nevertheless, while most respondents said they would be willing to talk openly about what happened to them or their families (63%), only half of these (30%) said they would feel safe or very safe doing so. Among those who said they would not want to talk openly about their experiences, half justified their position because they feared reprisal or revenge, whereas others justified not talking because they said it would be useless (24%).

In sum, although justice was a relatively remote priority for respondents, they nonetheless saw accountability as necessary to achieve a lasting peace. There was a strong preference for judicial means (whether national or international), but some significant interest in non-judicial mechanisms to achieve accountability (truth seeking, traditional justice, other conflict-resolution mechanisms). Despite the majority's (68%) willingness to "forgive" or reintegrate war criminals if this were the only way to achieve peace, 62 percent still preferred obtaining peace with justice over peace with forgiveness.

In a country with limited means of telecommunication, radio programs were, unsurprisingly, the primary source of information for the respondents.

- Fifty-four percent of respondents listened to the radio on a daily basis.

- For 67 percent, it was the primary source of information, followed by family and the community in general (23%).

- Most respondents trusted the radio moderately (27%), a lot (26%), or extremely (5%), although fewer believed journalists were moderately free (24%), very free (16%), or extremely free (3%) to report on social and political issues.

Survey Results from Kinshasa and Kisangani

The surveys conducted in Kinshasa and Kisangani show the extent to which people living in those two cities have also been affected by the war.

- A majority of respondents in Kinshasa (65%) and Kisangani (61%) identified themselves as victims of the conflicts, although at a lower level than those in eastern Congo (80%).

- Respondents in Kinshasa, Kisangani, and eastern Congo defined peace in similar terms and also saw it predominantly as the role of the Congolese government to bring peace. Yet respondents in Kinshasa were more frequently convinced that the stakeholders were committed to achieving peace (76%) compared to Kisangani (54%) and eastern Congo (58%).

- The priorities of respondents in the East, Kinshasa, and Kisangani diverge. Fifty-seven percent of respondents in Kinshasa and 47 percent in Kisangani identified the economy or employment as one of their priorities, compared to 15 percent in the East. Respondents in Kinshasa and Kisangani also more frequently identified food and education as priorities compared to those in the East. By contrast, respondents identified security as a priority more frequently in the East (34%) compared to Kisangani (22%) and Kinshasa (5%). Peace was identified as a priority more frequently in both the East (51%) and Kisangani (56%) than in Kinshasa (32%). These results were also reflected in the priorities respondents identified for the government.

- Respondents in all regions placed great importance on the need for accountability for those who committed grave crimes. When asked directly what should happen to those who committed these crimes, respondents in Kinshasa (41%) and Kisangani (39%) said more frequently that they wanted to see them in court than did respondents in eastern Congo (25%).

- Regarding how to achieve justice, respondents in Kinshasa opted more frequently for trials in international courts abroad (20%) compared to those in Kisangani (9%), and eastern Congo (7%). They also had more frequently heard about the ICC and the Lubanga proceedings.

RECOMMENDATIONS

TO THE CONGOLESE GOVERNMENT

- Implement the recent peace negotiations addressing security concerns with belligerents in the East. In light of the destabilizing potential of ongoing conflict in eastern DRC, peace and security remain prerequisites for future economic development.

- Undertake effective reform of the security sector, not only to ensure that past human rights violators are removed from the ranks, but also to train the national police and army to be human rights protectors rather than violators whom civilians fear, as is the current perception of the population.

- Open an inter-community dialogue to address social antagonisms, resolve underlying causes of the conflicts including access to land and exploitation of natural resources, facilitate the demobilization and reintegration of former combatants, and permit the return of internally displaced and refugees.

- Develop a broad-based reconstruction plan that engages the population and reflects the priorities expressed by the respondents.

- Commit to national dialogue with population to assess various transitional justice mechanisms, including prosecutions and other reconciliation mechanisms, such as inter-ethnic dialogue to address root causes of the conflict.

- Engage in effective reform of the national judicial sector including
  - Reform of military and civilian court systems to guarantee independence, transparency, and due process to build trust in the judicial system.
  - Prioritize the prosecution of war crimes and ensure national complementarity with the ICC by adopting an effective legislative framework for national prosecutions of war crimes.
  - End impunity for crimes of rape and sexual violence.

TO THE INFORMAL AND FORMAL BELLIGERENTS ACTIVE IN EASTERN DRC

- Respect the ceasefire terms of recent peace agreements and engage in an effective process of demobilization, disarmament, and reintegration. The government of Rwanda should engage in meaningful collaboration for the disarmament, demobilization, and repatriation of Rwandan Hutu FDLR combatants on DRC soil.

TO BILATERAL AND MULTILATERAL INTERNATIONAL DONORS

- Maintain pressure on the DRC government and belligerents to respect the peace process; monitor and ensure respect for the ceasefire.

- Ensure that the DRC government and belligerents pursue peace and justice simultaneously by including commitments that guarantee accountability and the pursuit of a multifaceted approach to transitional justice mechanisms in ongoing peace processes.

- Focus on international engagement with reforming the national judicial sector to promote accountability for human rights violations and the rule of law. Transitional justice concerns should be integrated into judicial reform plans.

- Oversee government security sector reform to guarantee transitional justice concerns are met, including vetting and an effective disciplinary system for ongoing human rights violations committed by army and police.

- Engage in a long-term development strategy to promote good governance of Congolese state institutions.

TO MONUC AND UNITED NATIONS ENTITIES

- The United Nations Security Council must renew the mandate of MONUC to continue to engage in monitoring peace in eastern DRC.

- MONUC should ensure that it implements its mandate to protect civilians.

- The Office of the High Commissioner for Human Rights (OHCHR) should effectively complete its mandate to conduct a six-month mapping exercise of human rights violations and should engage in broad-based consultations of the Congolese population to seek additional information regarding the population's needs and preferences for pursuing various transitional justice mechanisms.

TO THE INTERNATIONAL CRIMINAL COURT

- Improve its information campaign and outreach for upcoming trials, taking advantage of radio as a means of disseminating information.

- Review the possibility of holding its trials *in situ*.

- Continue and broaden the investigation and prosecution of suspected war criminals.

AUTHORS AND ACKNOWLEDGEMENTS

Patrick Vinck and Phuong Pham led the design and development of the survey in eastern Congo, Kinshasa, and Kisangani. Patrick Vinck, Phuong Pham, Suliman Baldo, and Rachel Shigekane wrote the report.* Eric Stover at the Human Rights Center, University of California, Berkeley, and Alpha Fall at the International Center for Transitional Justice contributed to the research. The report benefited from input by Mirna Adjami, Cecile Aptel, Richard Bailey, Laura Davis, Virginie Ladish, Graeme Simpson, and Marieke Wierda at the International Center for Transitional Justice. Camille Crittenden and Barbara Grob from the Human Rights Center, University of California, Berkeley, edited the report.

We wish to thank our field coordinators and surveyors for their dedication and work in difficult situations, and colleagues at the School of Public Health at the University of Kinshasa for their help coordinating the study. For confidentiality reasons, individual acknowledgements will not be listed here. However, this report would not have been possible without their support. We also wish to thank the survey respondents for taking the time to share their views with us. We thank Pamela Blotner for her original illustration used on the cover.

The research and report were supported by grants from the John D. and Catherine T. MacArthur Foundation, Humanity United, Swedish International Development Cooperation, the European Commission, and the BBC World Service Trust. The information provided and views expressed in this publication can in no way be taken to represent the official opinion of the funding agencies.

PATRICK VINCK is the Director of the Berkeley-Tulane Initiative for Vulnerable Populations at the University of California, Berkeley and Adjunct Professor at the Payson Center for International Development, Tulane University (pvinck@berkeley.edu).

PHUONG PHAM is a Research Associate Professor at the Payson Center for International Development, Tulane University and a Senior Research Fellow at the Human Rights Center of the University of California, Berkeley (ppham1@tulane.edu).

SULIMAN BALDO is Director of the Africa Program at the International Center for Transitional Justice (sbaldo@ictj.org).

RACHEL SHIGEKANE is Program Director at the Human Rights Center, University of California, Berkeley (rshig@berkeley.edu).

CPSIA information can be obtained at www.ICGtesting.com
Printed in the USA
BVOW050826151111

276124BV00006B/1/P